Published by ©Piano Notion
1st edition 2019 / revised 2022
www.pianonotion.com

Author: Bobby Cyr

Graphic design: Imagine Design

Logo: Studio Azura

Revision and communication: Marie-France Palardy

Translation: Traductions Kaizen

U.K revision: Ellie Jaggers and Emma Palmer

Legal deposit: Bibliothèque nationale du Québec, 2022

Legal deposit: Library and Archives Canada, 2022

ISMN: 979-0-9001551-7-7

Presentation

This piano method contains a collection of pieces and may also be used as a repertoire book. The method gives students the opportunity to build on prior learning and fully assimilate the material as the pieces become increasingly difficult.

Musical concepts are presented one at a time, with examples and exercises provided in the Appendices. Students then put these new concepts into practice as they learn and perform the pieces, further exploring and assimilating the new ideas and skills.

Book two introduces dotted rhythms, accidentals and the keys of F and G. Major and minor chords are also introduced in several of the pieces. Students will learn different left hand accompaniment patterns to go along with the beautiful melodies.

The repertoire

The repertoire was carefully selected from among the most beautiful songs from around the world. The date of composition as well as the country of origin of each song is indicated along with the title. The composer's name is also given, and if the composer is unknown, a Roud number is provided. The Roud Folk Song Index is a database of songs collected from oral tradition from all over the world.

Music reading exercises

Rhythm and note reading exercises are provided in the Appendices. They are listed by order of difficulty to help students develop their music reading skills.

Copyright and intellectual property

For more information, visit: www.pianonotion.com

Table of Contents

Level 5 pieces

New concepts

1- Changing left hand position on the keyboard

2- Flats

3- Sharps

4- Naturals

From now on, the pieces are no longer in C position only. Before playing, carefully look at the notes and place your hands in the correct starting position.

Bahay Kubo

Philippines (1924)

Unknown composer
Arr. Bobby Cyr

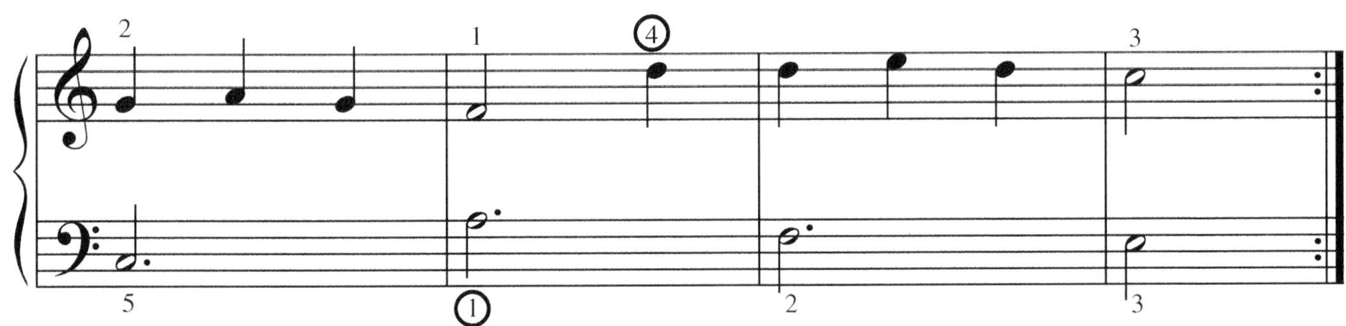

Flats

A flat ♭ indicates that a note is played one half step (semitone) lower.

See Appendix 2 (page 81) for whole steps and half steps (tones and semitones).

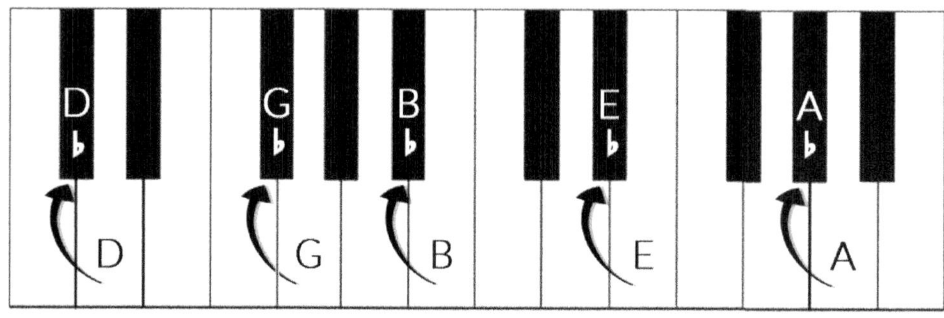

In a piece, the flat ♭ symbol is always placed in front of the note.

Example: ♭♩

The flat applies to any following notes on the same line or space in the measure.

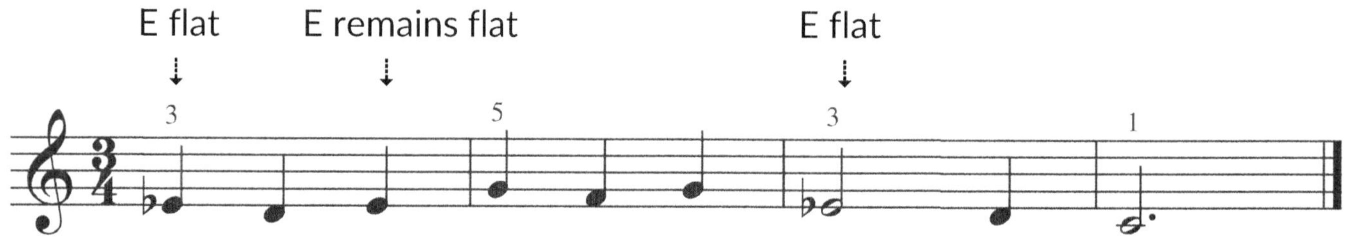

The flat no longer applies in the next measure.

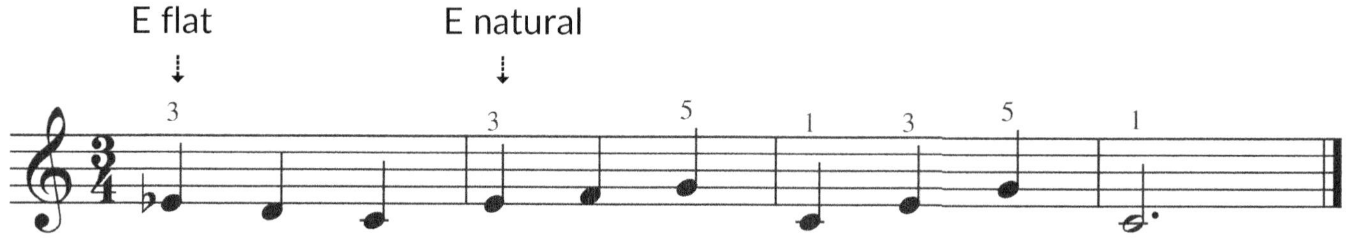

Michael Finnegan

Ireland (1868)

Unknown composer
Roud 13512
Arr. Bobby Cyr

♩ = 112

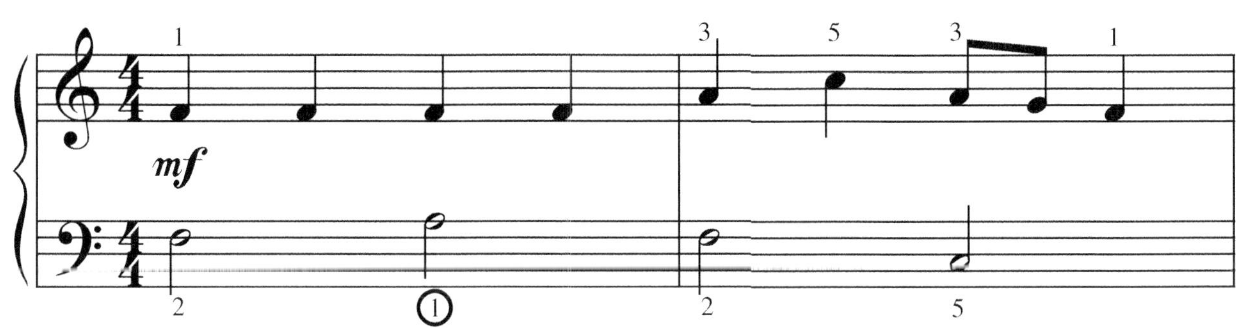

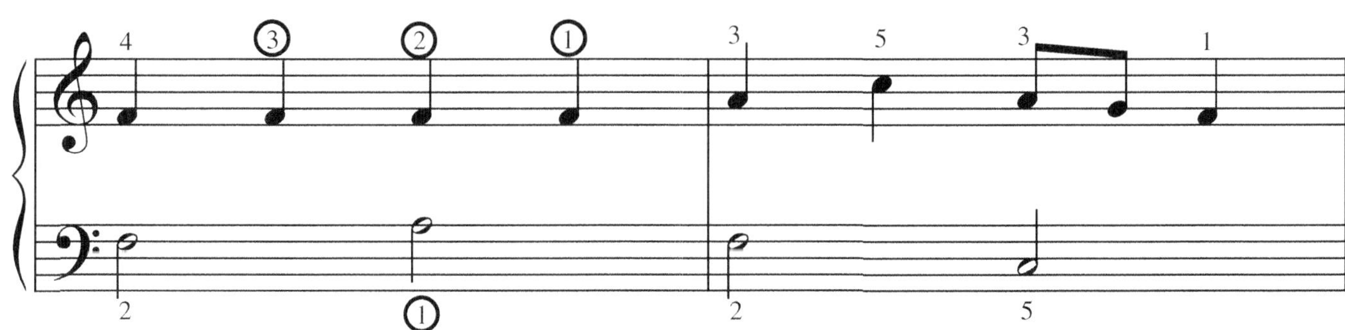

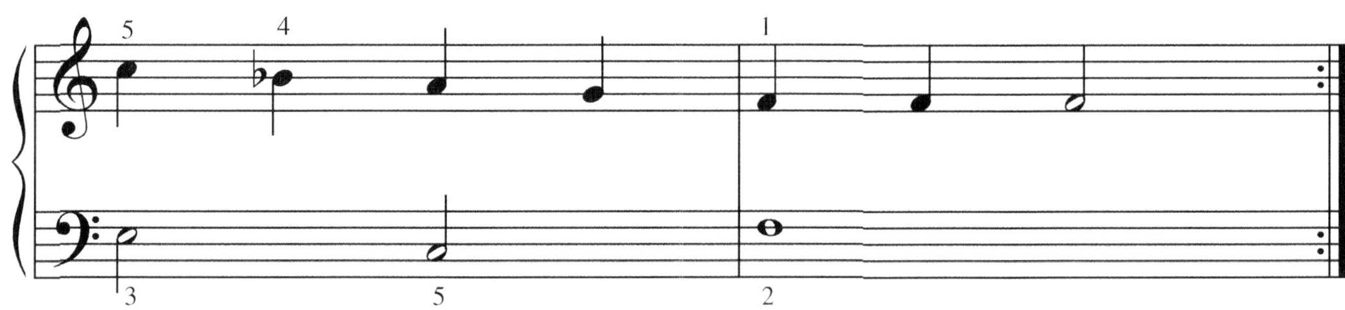

Sharps

A sharp ♯ indicates that a note is played one half step (semitone) higher.

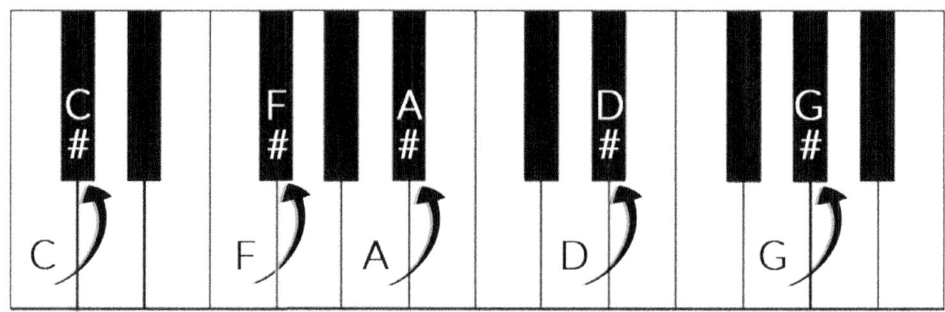

In a piece, the sharp symbol ♯ is always placed in front of the note.

Example : ♯♩

The sharp applies to any following notes on the same line or space in the measure.

The sharp no longer applies in the next measure.

Slavonic March

Russia (1876)

Pyotr Ilyich Tchaikovsky
(1840-1893)
Arr. Bobby Cyr

♩ = 120

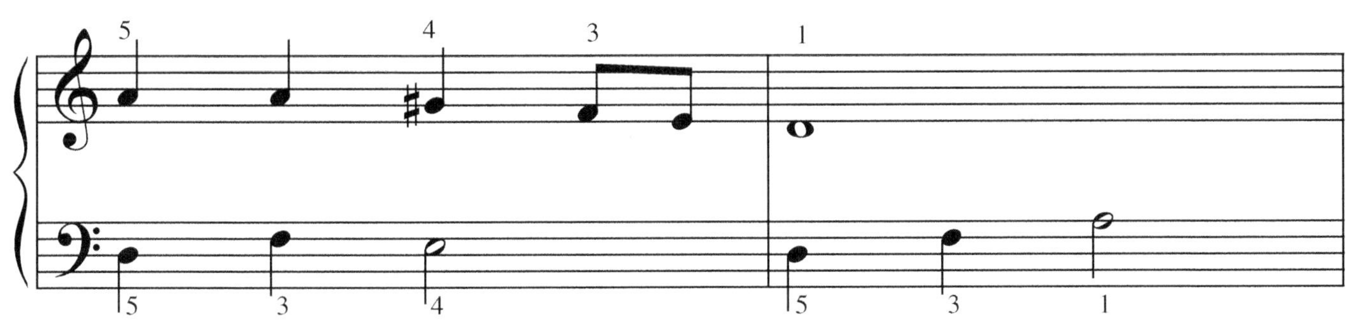

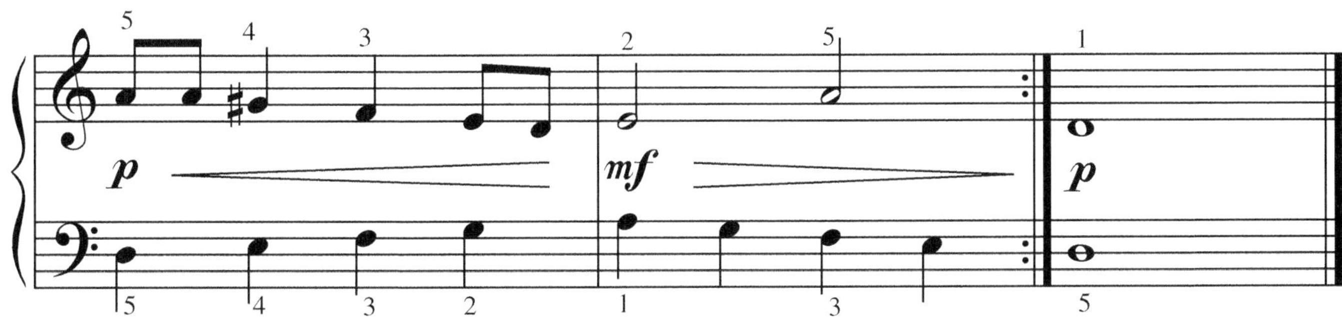

Egyptian dance

France

Camille Saint-Saëns
(1835-1921)
Arr. Bobby Cyr

♩ = 72

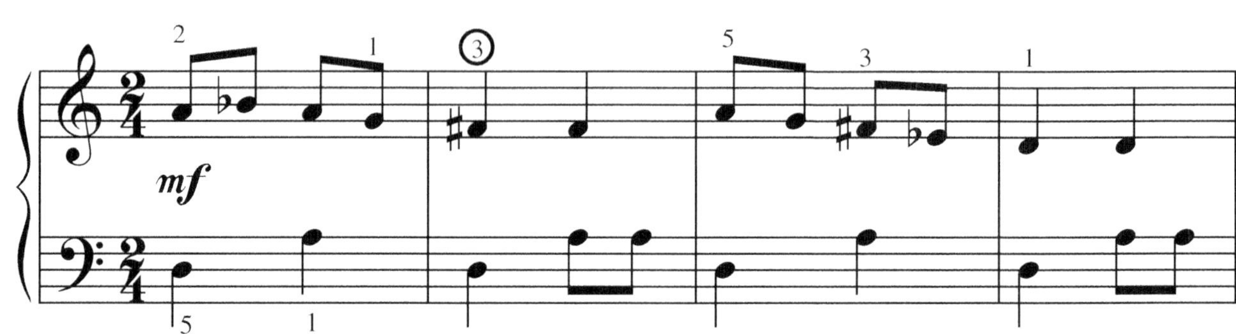

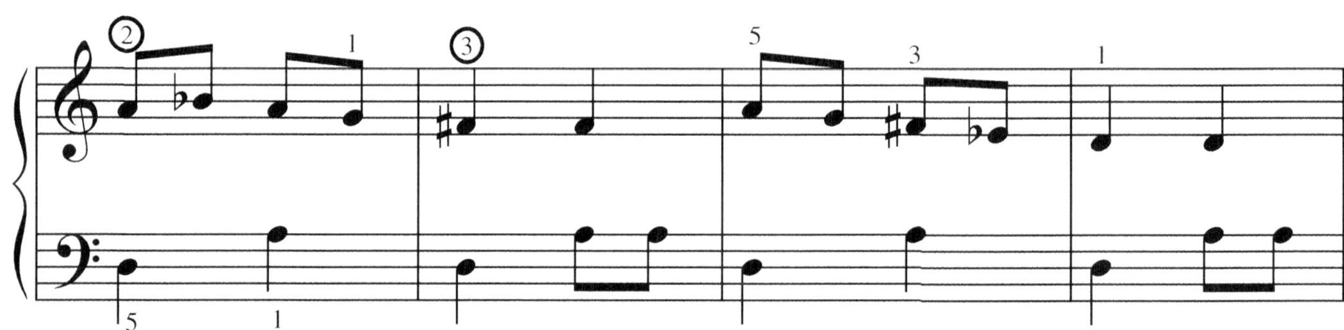

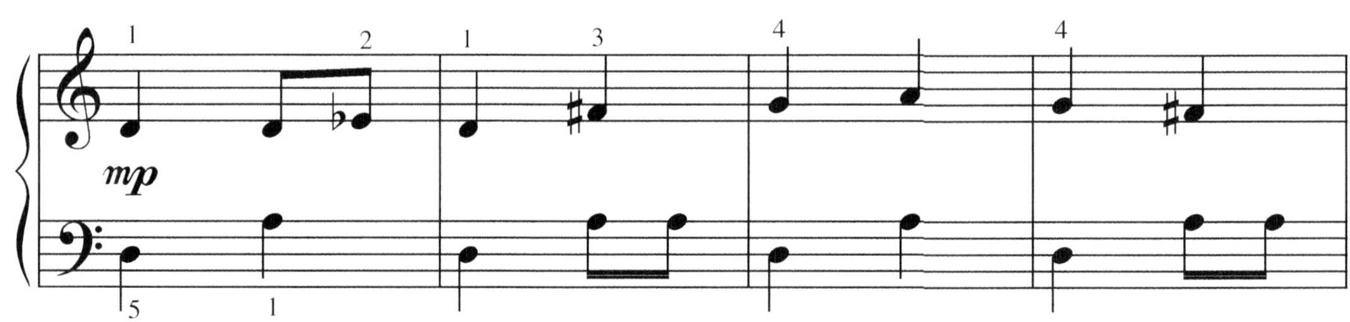

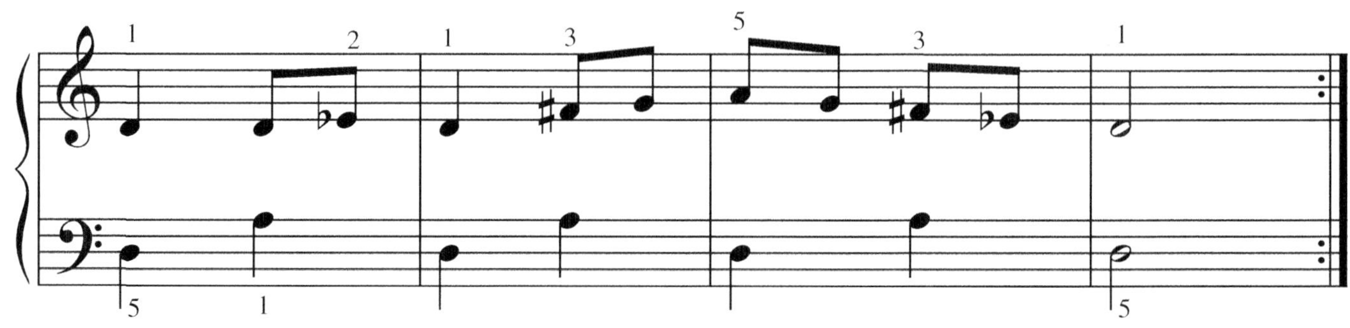

Naturals

A natural ♮ indicates that a note returns to its natural pitch.

In a piece, the natural symbol ♮ is also placed in front of the note.

Example: ♮♩

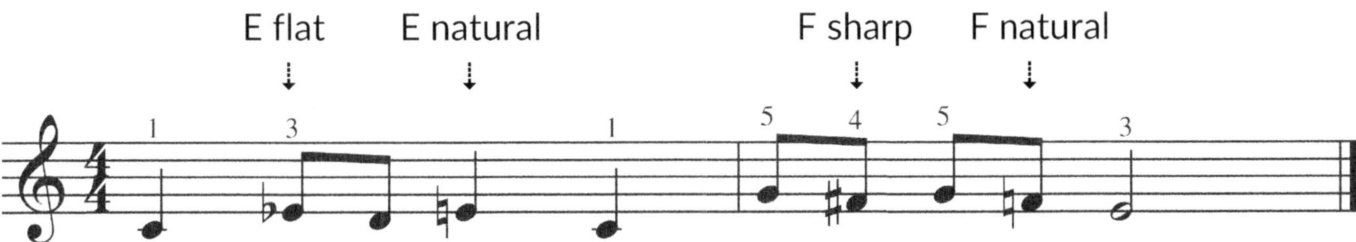

Cautionary naturals

Although accidentals (♭ and ♯), are cancelled once you reach a new measure, in some cases, a cautionary (or reminder) natural is provided.

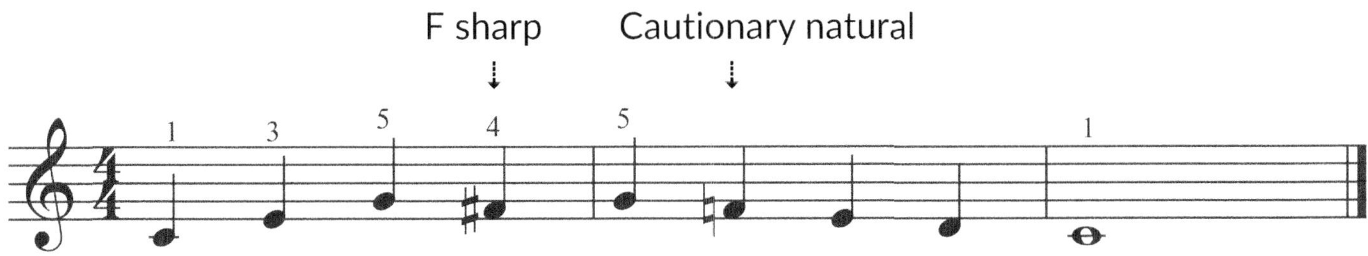

The Old Gray Mare

United States

Stephen Foster
(1826-1864)
Arr. Bobby Cyr

♩ = 112

In the Hall of the Mountain King

Norway

Edvard Grieg
(1843-1907)
Arr. Bobby Cyr

♩ = 88

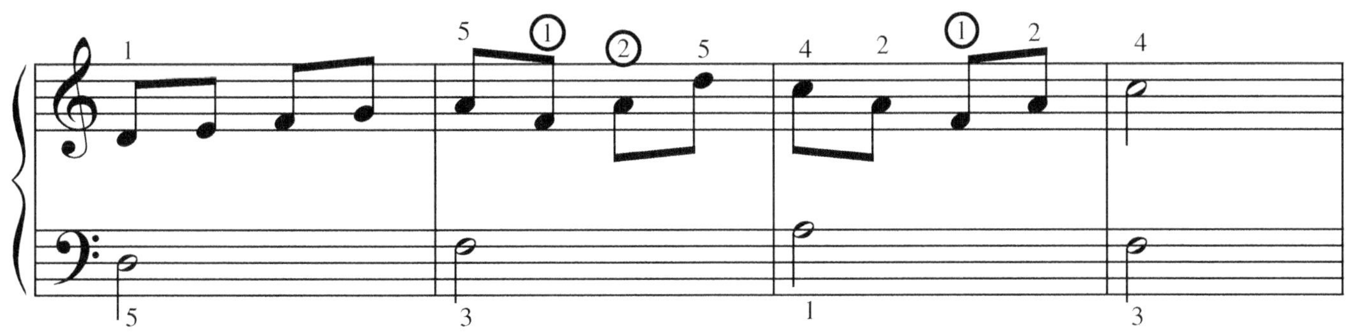

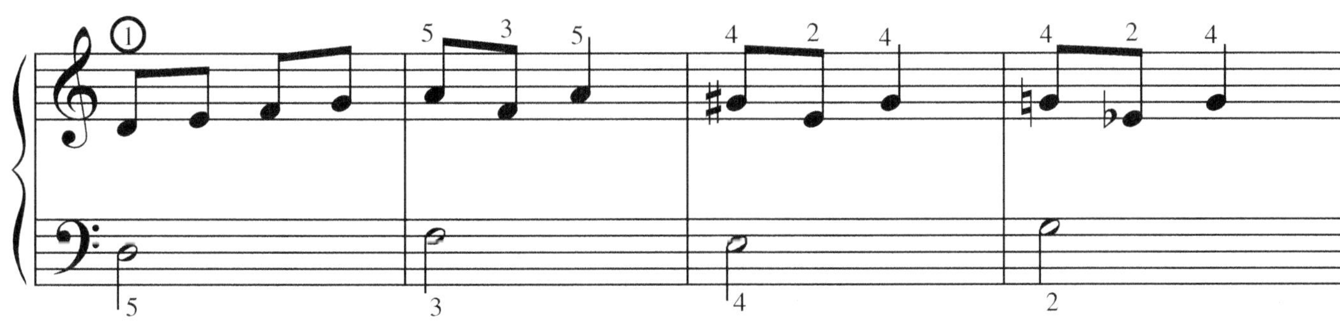

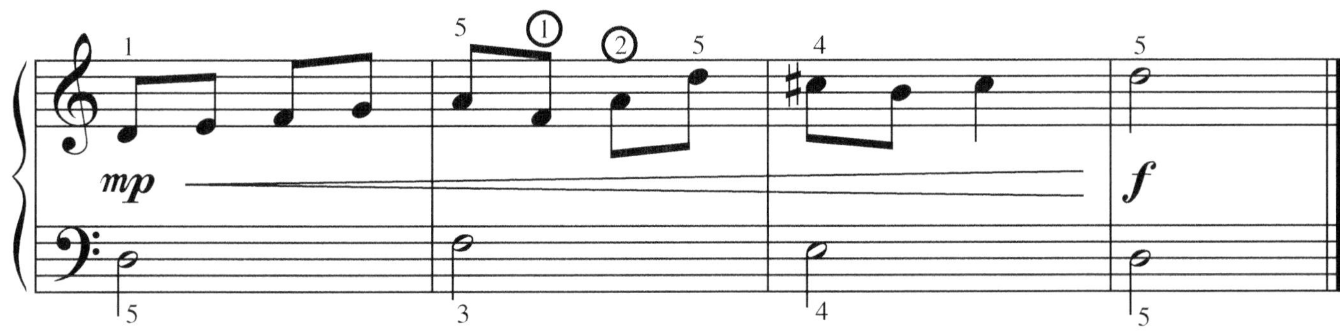

Level 6 pieces

Dotted quarter notes | Dotted crotchets

A dotted quarter note has a value equal to a quarter note tied to an eighth note.

The dot adds half of the value of the note to itself.
Count the beats with the (and).

1 and 2 1 and 2

A dotted quarter note is often followed by an eighth note.
The eighth note completes the second beat.

1 and 2 and 1 and 2 and

Exercise: see Appendix 1 (page 78)

From the New World

Czech republic (1893)

Antonin Dvorak
(1841-1904)
Arr. Bobby Cyr

♩ = 80

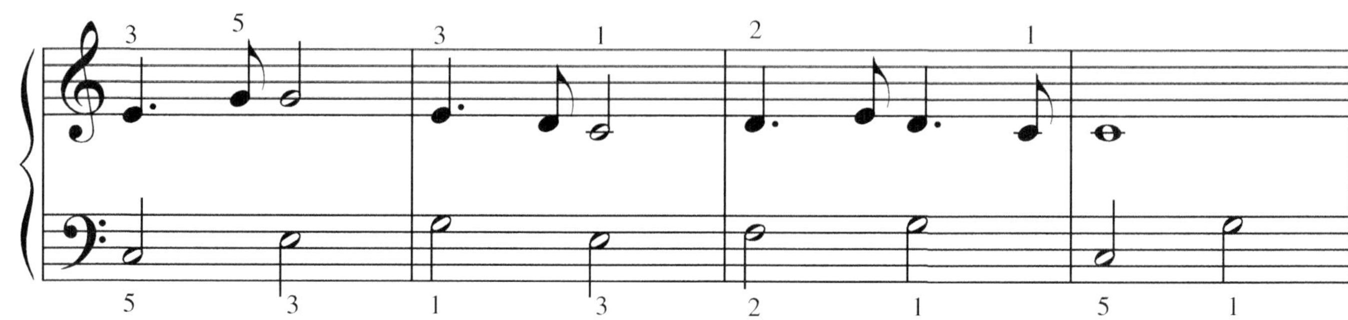

From the New World

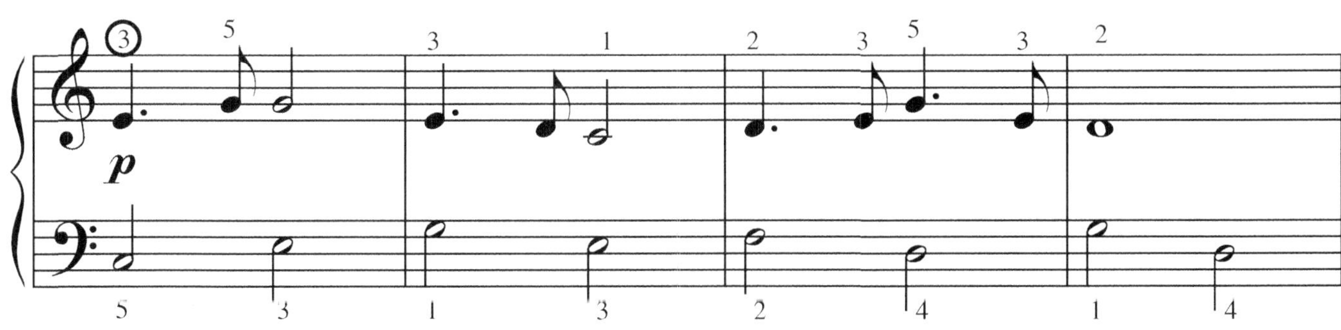

Mozart Sonata

Austria (1787)

Wolfgang Amadeus Mozart
(1756-1791)
Arr. Bobby Cyr

♩ = 100

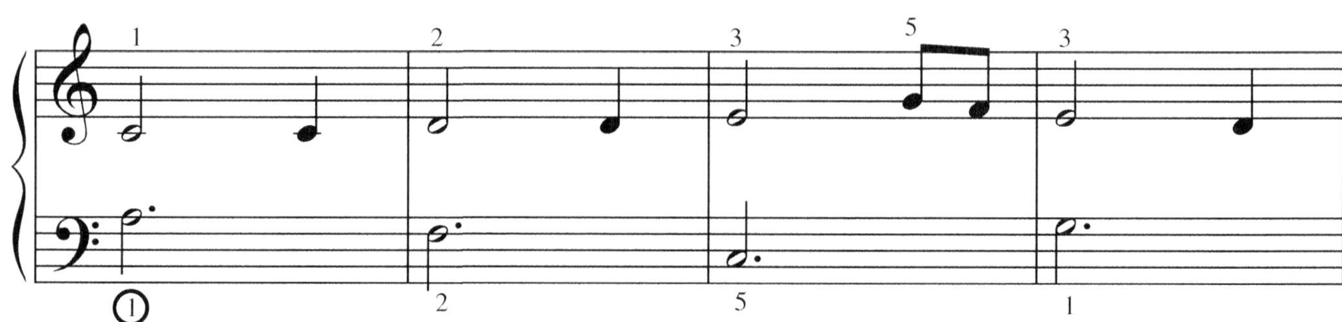

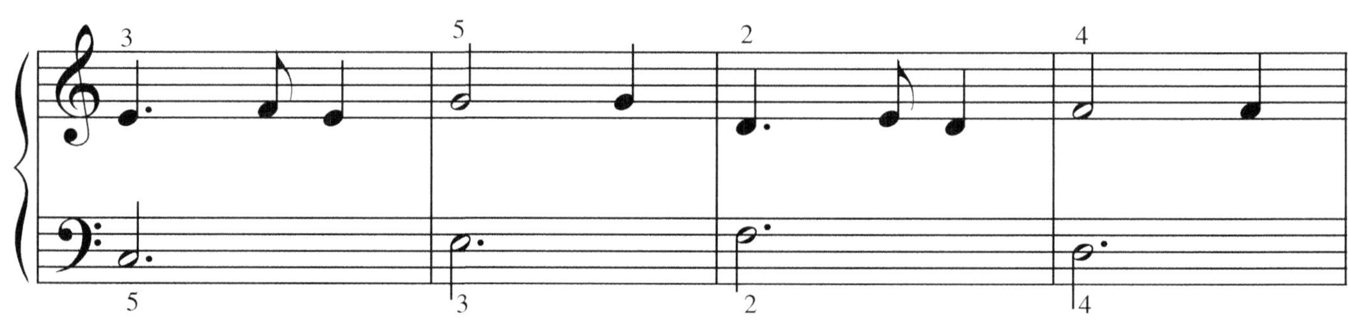

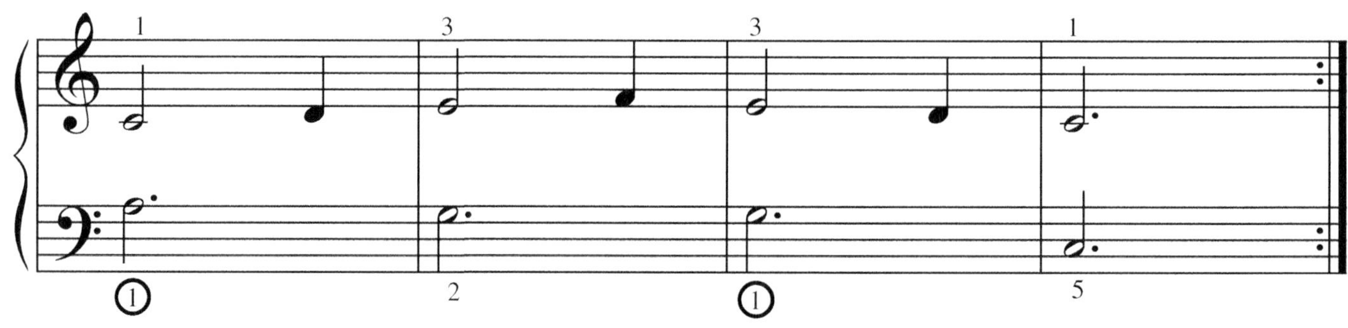

Ode to Joy

An die Freude
Austria (1824)

Ludwig van Beethoven
(1770-1827)
Arr. Bobby Cyr

♩ = 100

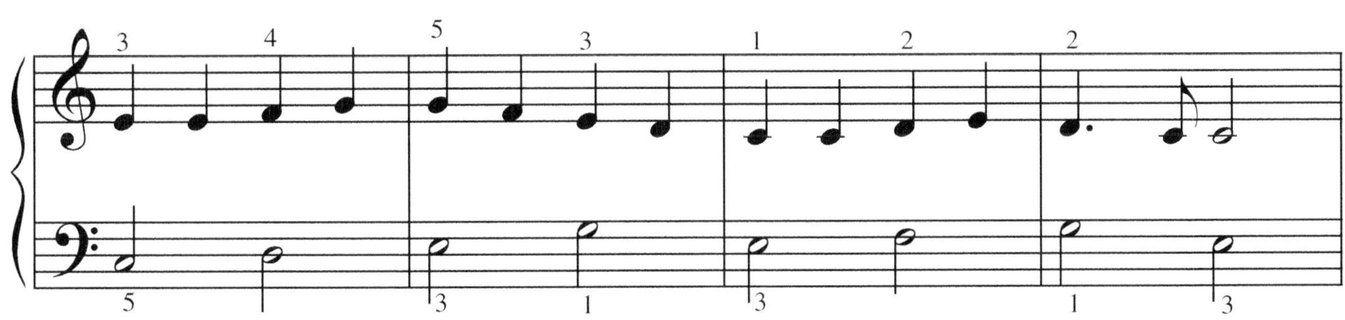

Oh! Susanna

United States (1848)

Stephen Foster
(1826-1864)
Arr. Bobby Cyr

♩ = 120

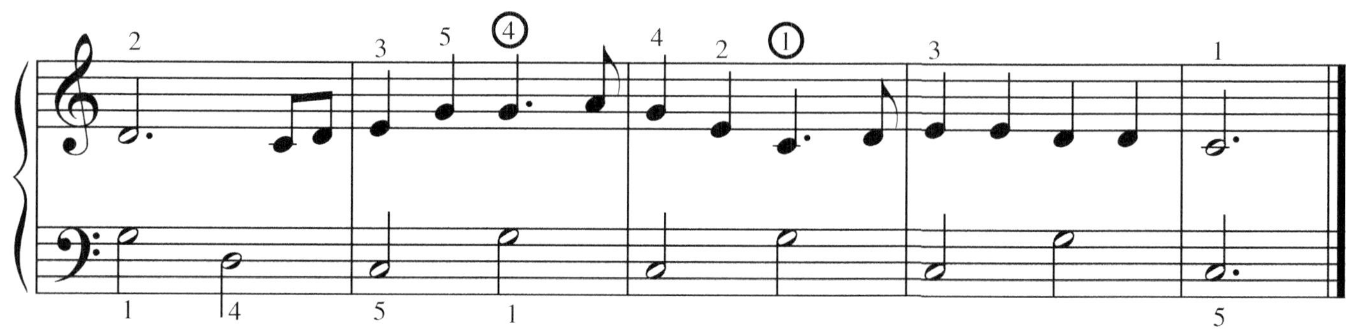

God Save the Queen

England (1619)

John Bull
(1562-1628)
Arr. Bobby Cyr

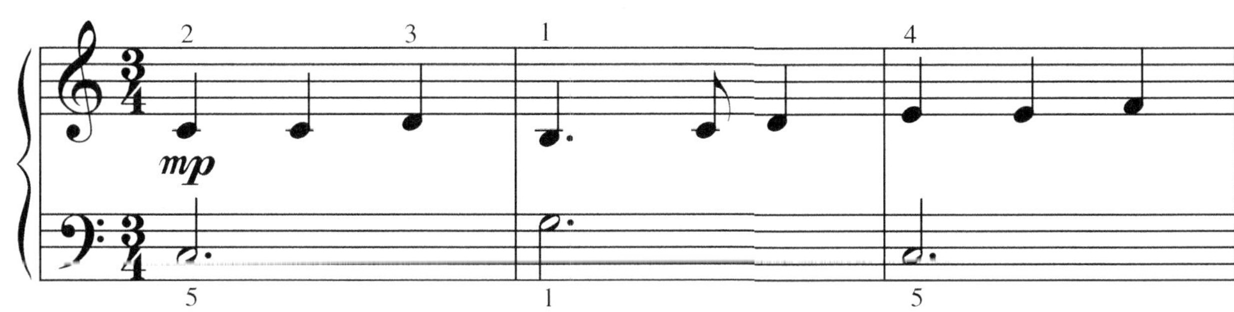

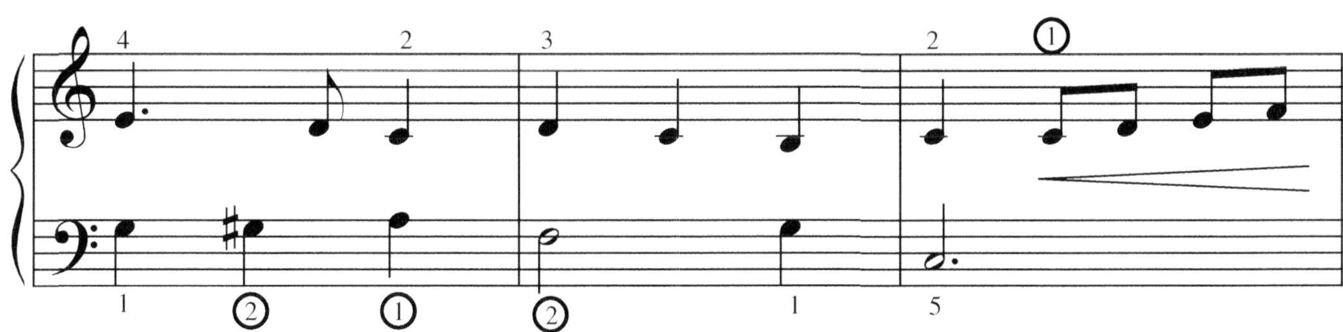

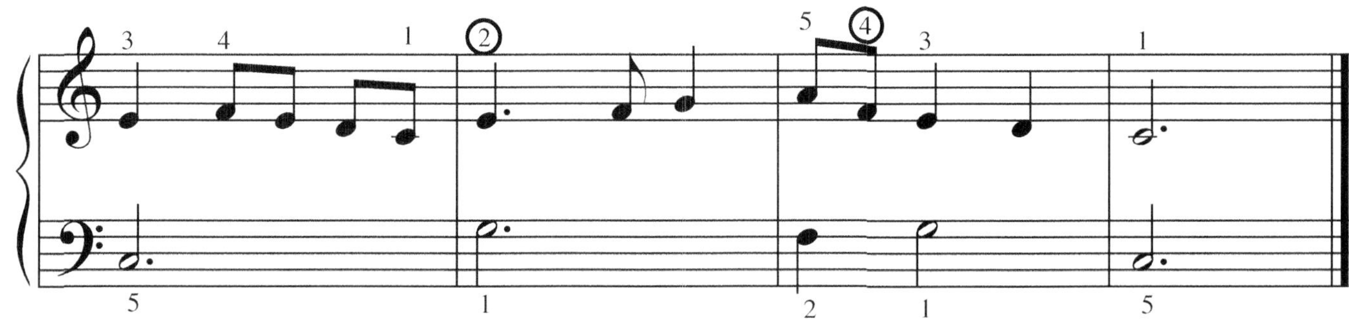

The Muffin Man

England (1820)

Unknown composer
Roud 7922
Arr. Bobby Cyr

♩ = 120

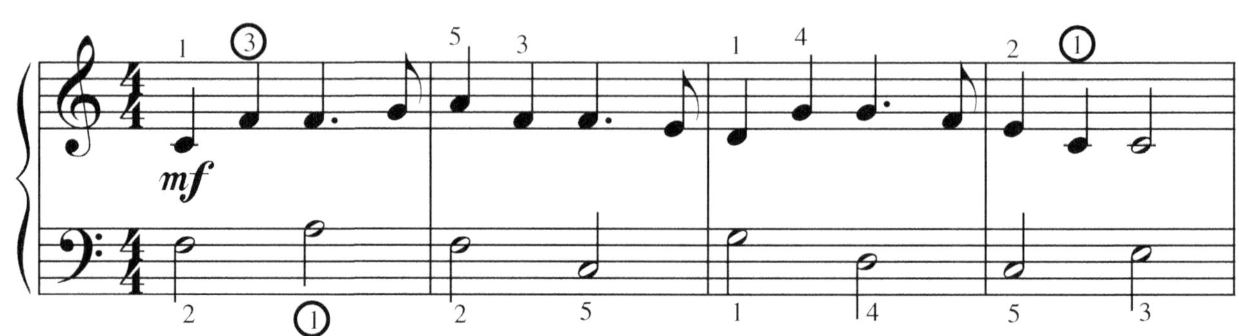

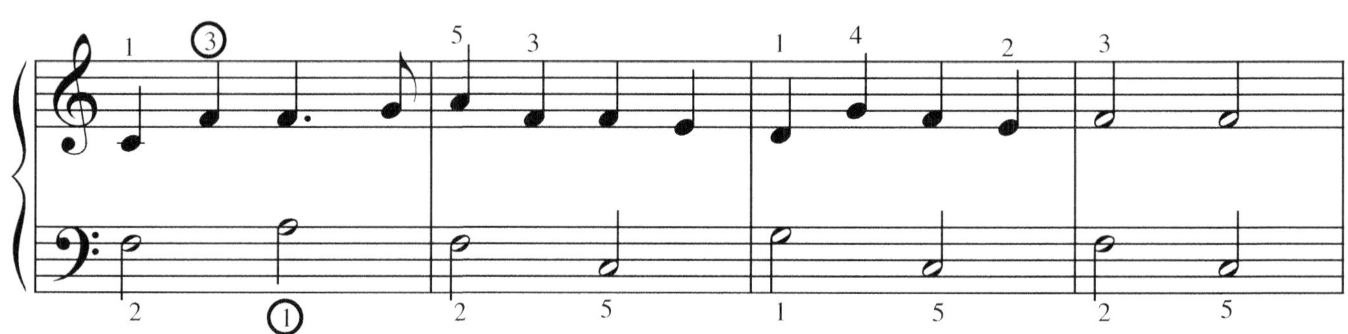

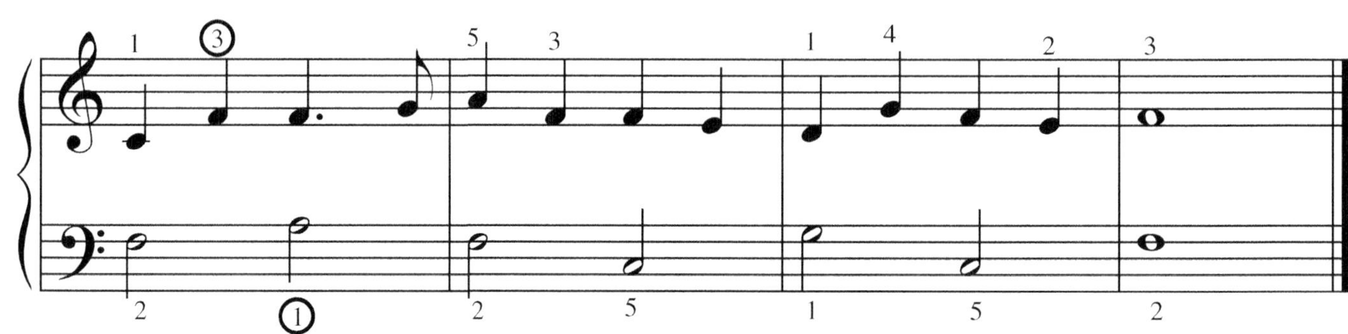

Oh, My Dear Augustin

Oh du lieber Augustin
Austria (1679)

Marx Augustin
(1685-1705)
Arr. Bobby Cyr

♩ = 112

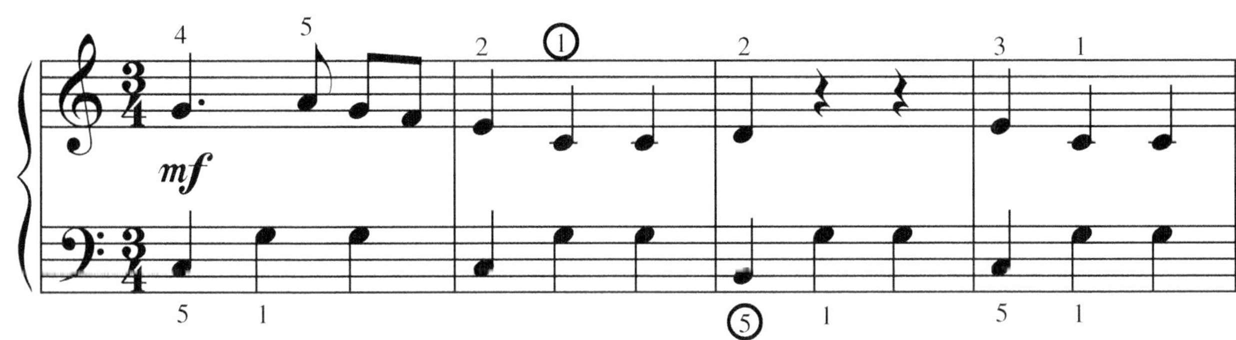

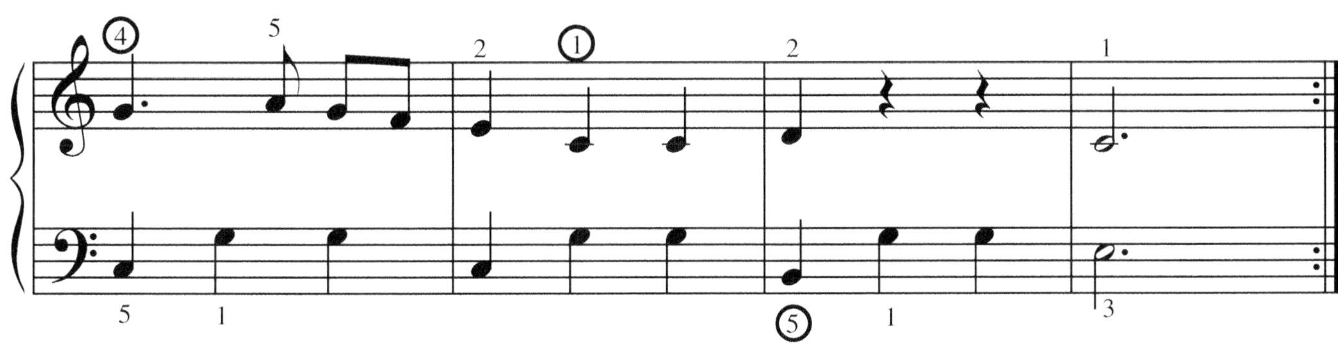

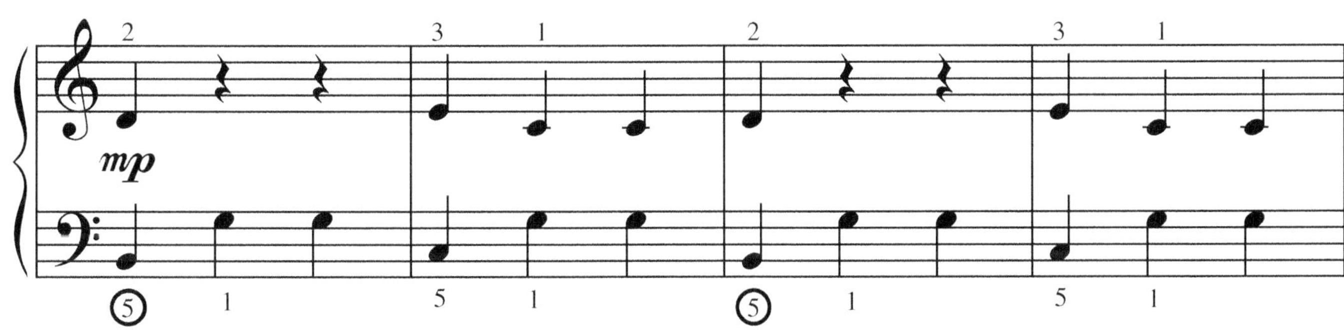

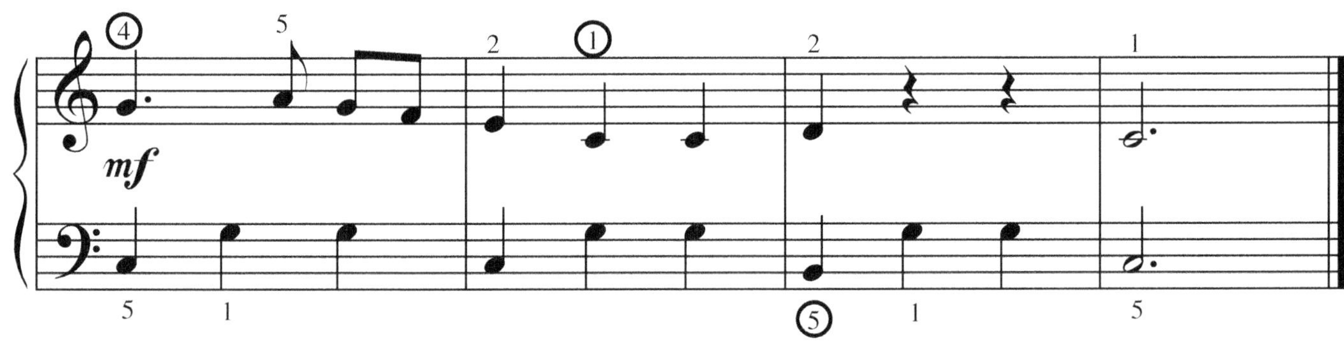

Schubert's Lullaby

Wiegenlied
Austria (1816)

Franz Schubert
(1797-1828)
Arr. Bobby Cyr

♩ = 92

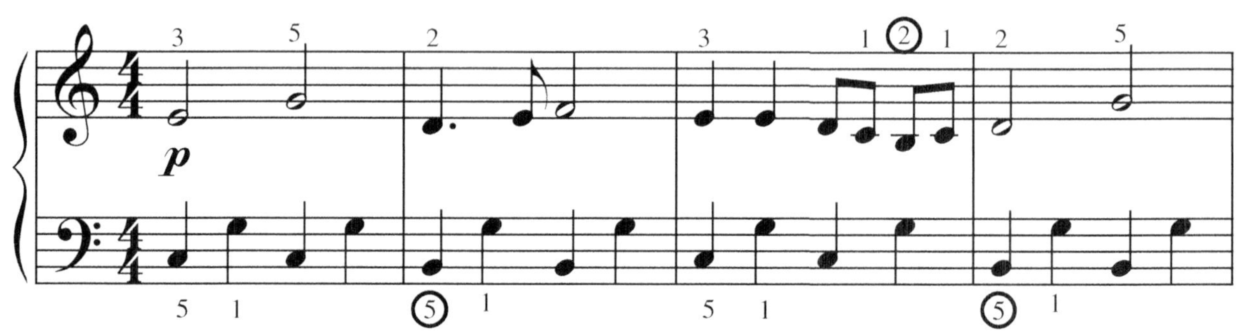

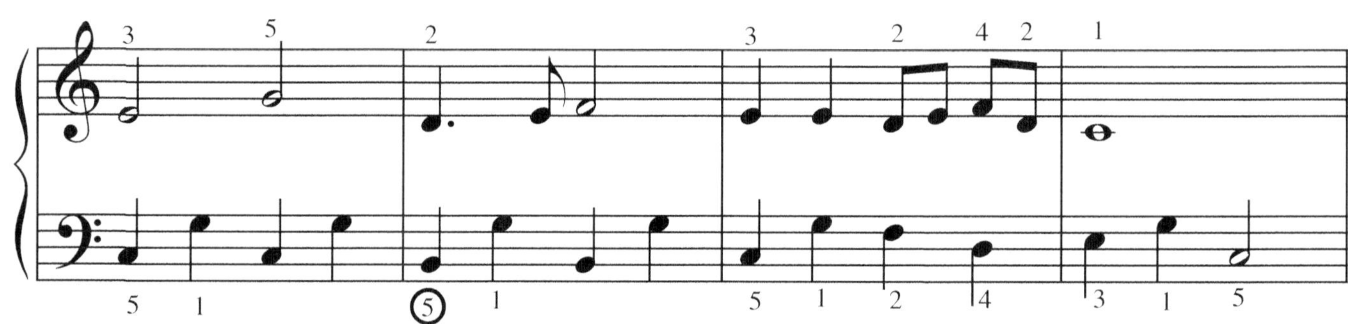

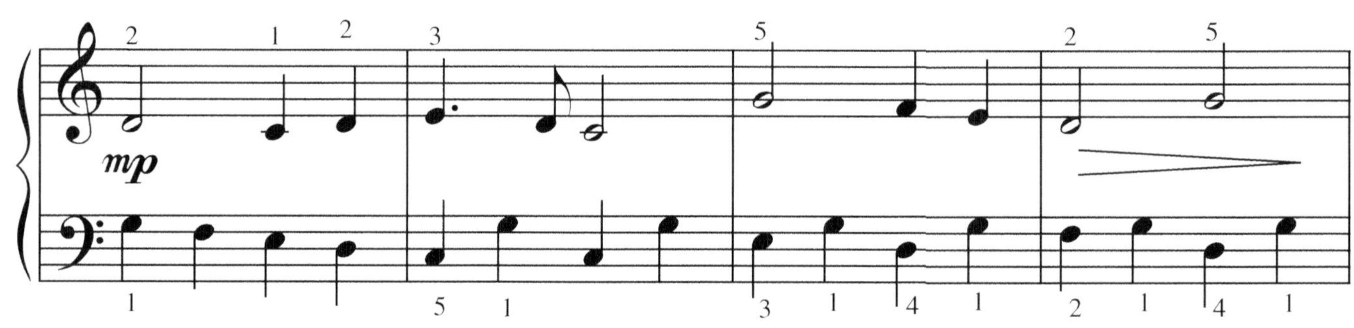

Level 7 pieces

Harmonic and melodic intervals

An interval is the distance between two notes.
Harmonic interval: notes played simultaneously.
Melodic interval: notes played successively.

Unison

Second

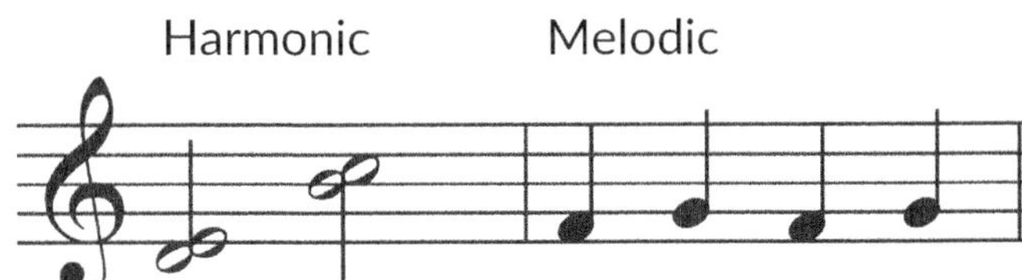

Third

Fourth

Fifth

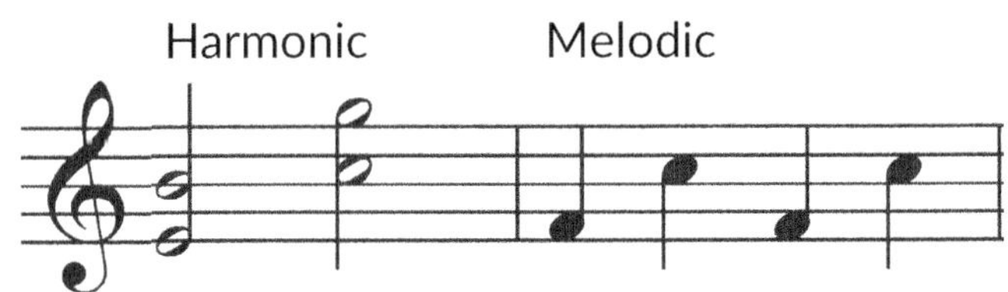

Sixth

Seventh

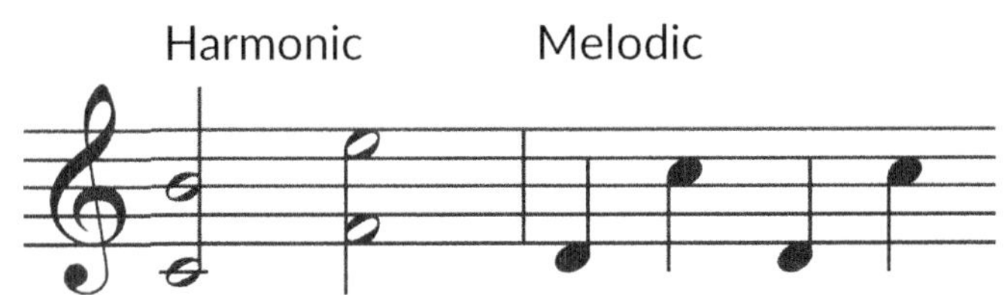

Octave

Harmony

In a piece, notes lined up vertically are played simultaneously.

Example: whole notes half notes quarter notes

Exercise: Play the intervals with the left hand.

Michael Row the Boat Ashore

United States (1860)

Unknown composer
Roud 11975
Arr. Bobby Cyr

♩ = 100

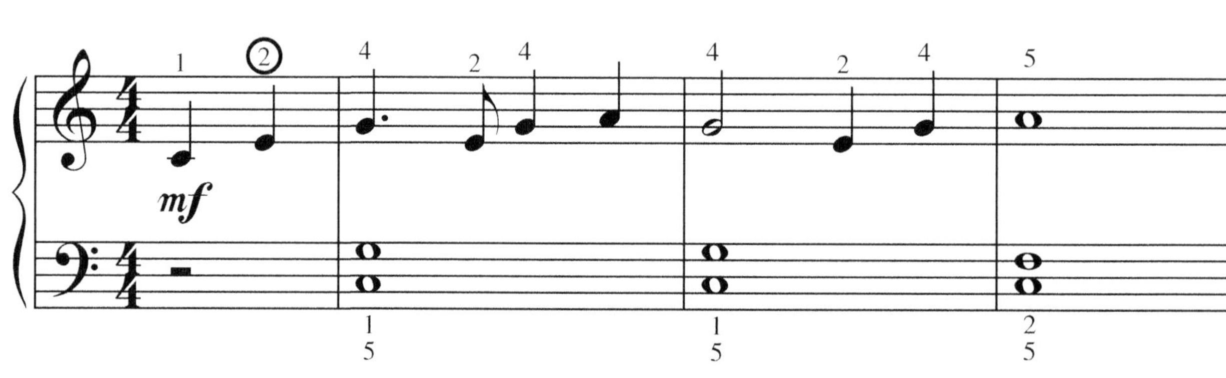

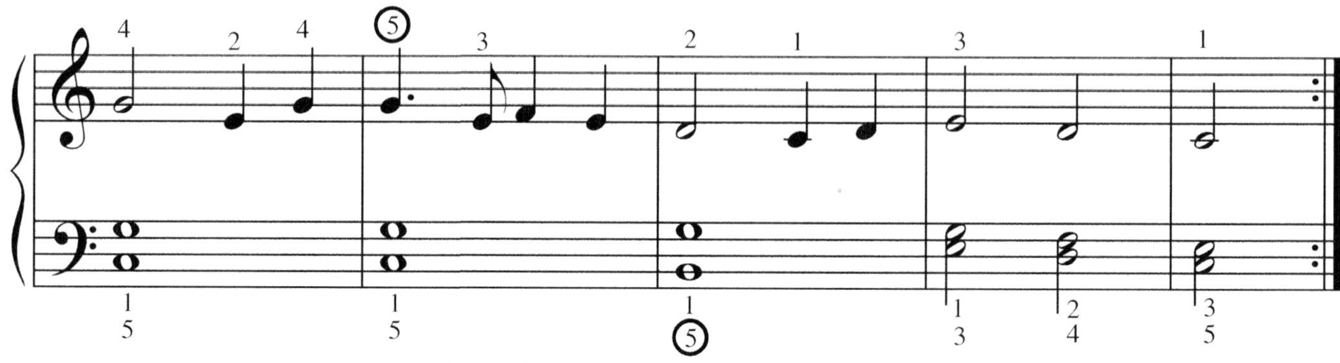

Ani couni

Ani'qu ne'chawu'nani'
Canada

Unknown composer
Arr. Bobby Cyr

♩ = 80

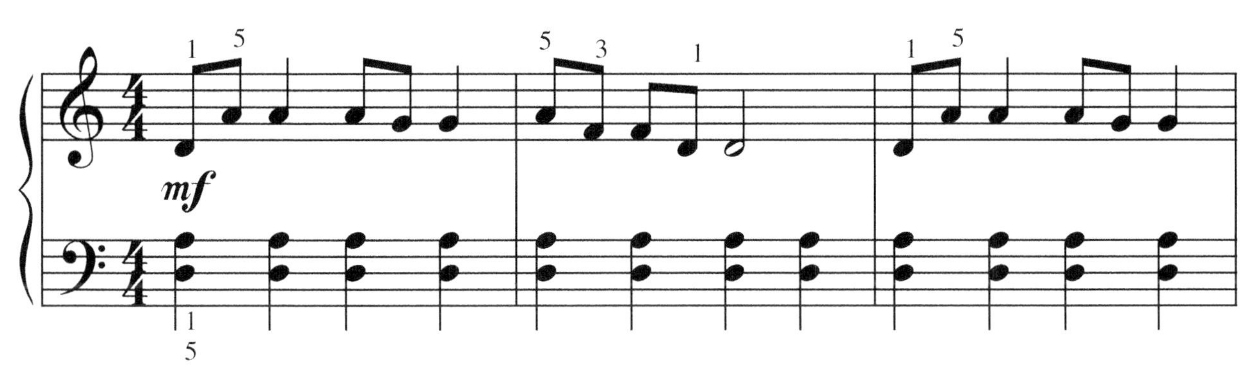

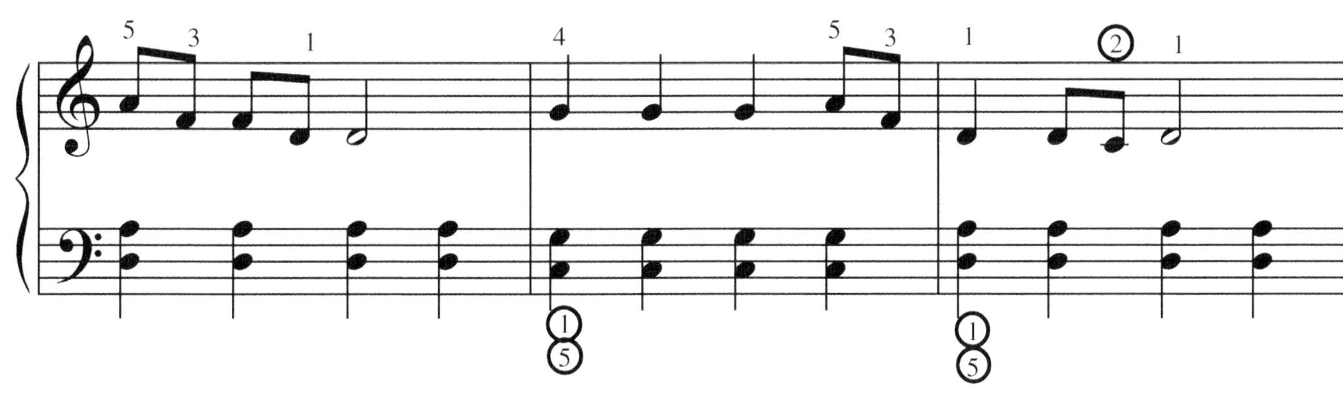

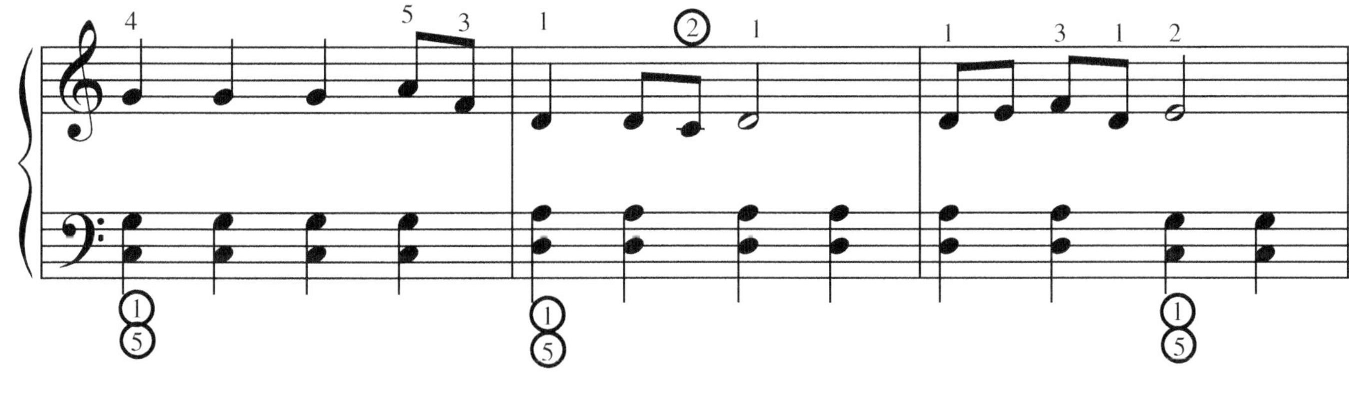

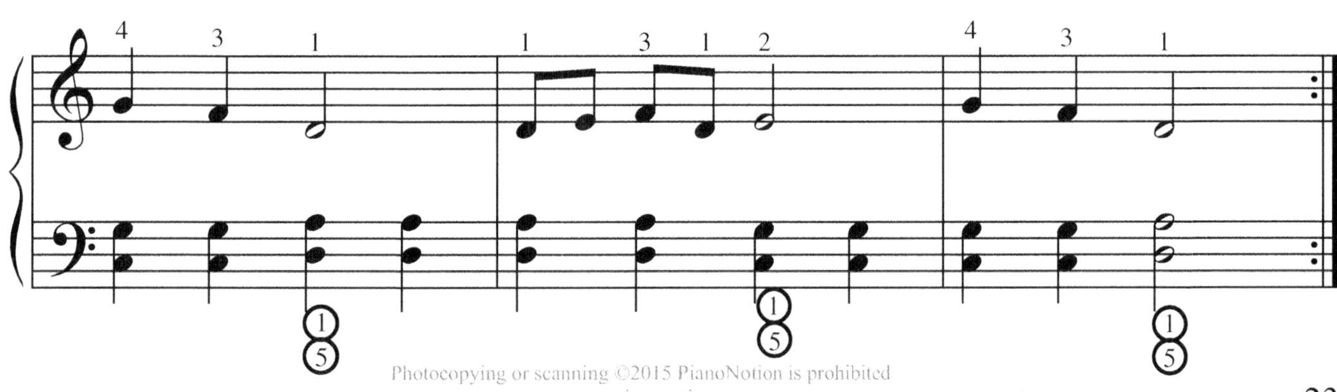

Spring

La primavera
Italy (1725)

Antonio Lucio Vivaldi
(1678-1741)
Arr. Bobby Cyr

♩ = 112

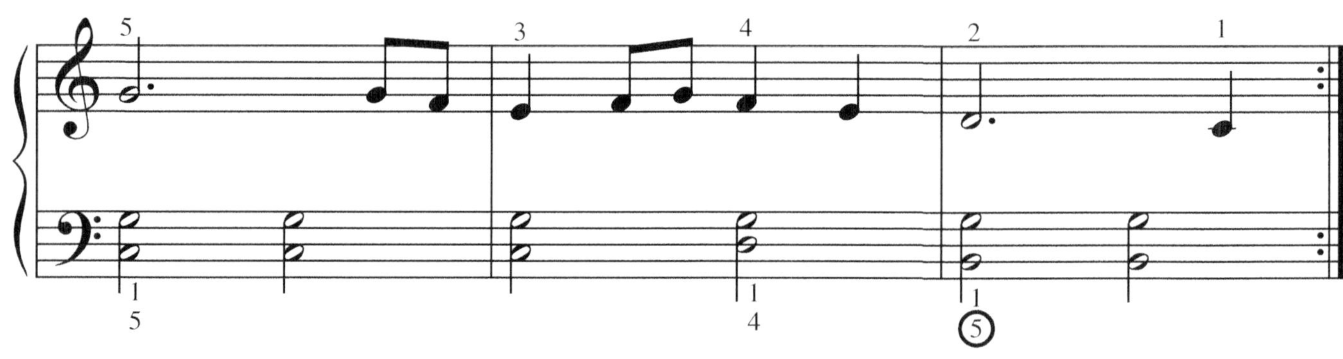

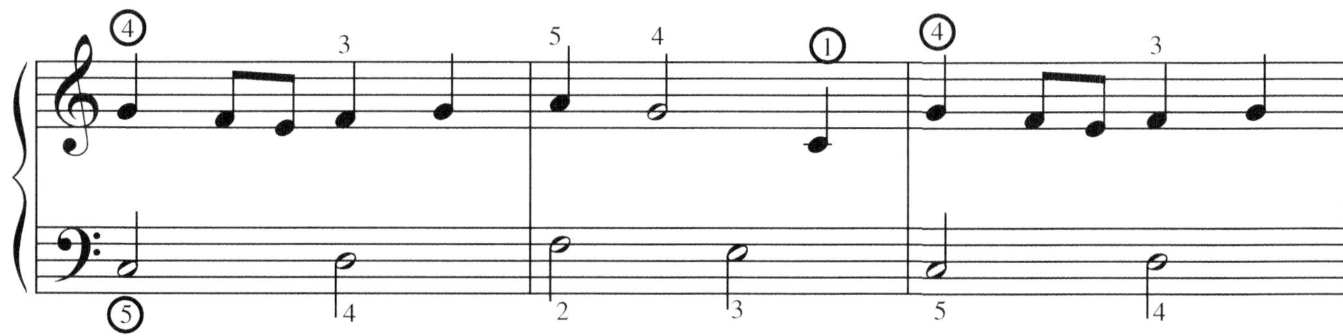

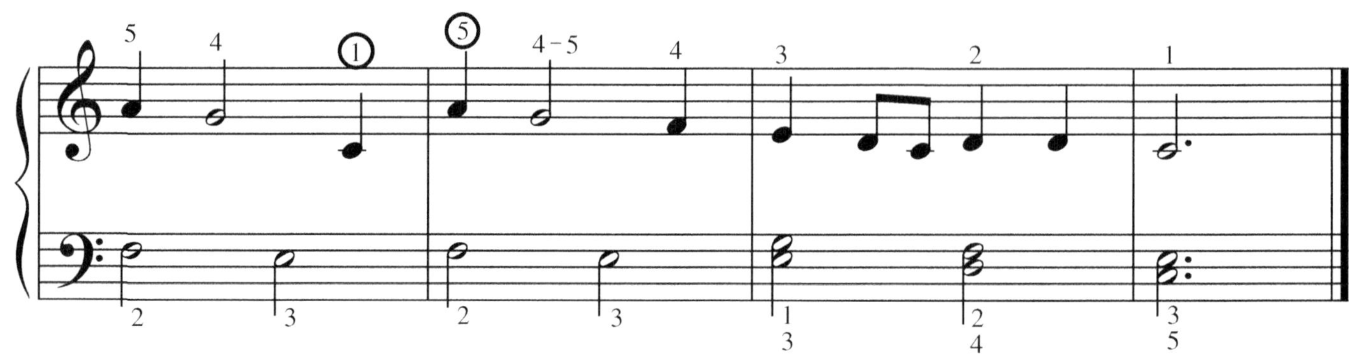

Chopsticks

Great Britain (1877)

Euphemia Allen
(1861-1949)
Arr. Bobby Cyr

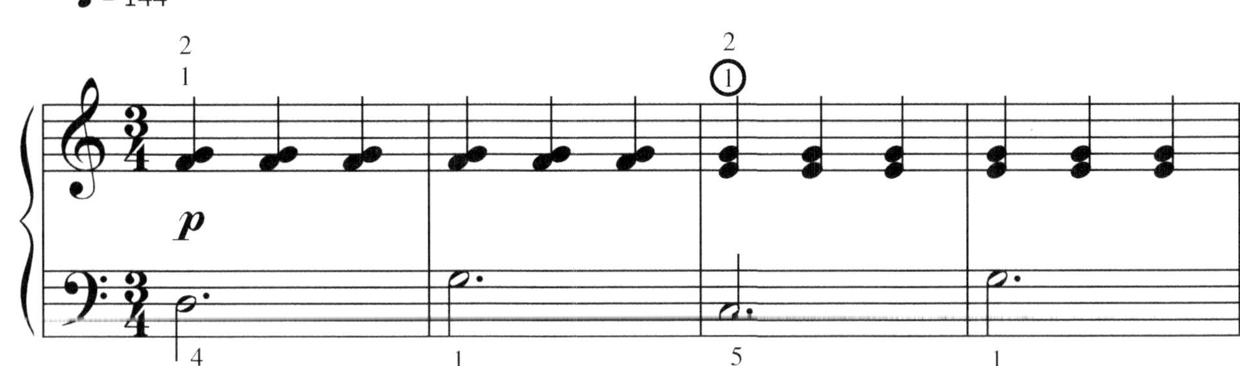

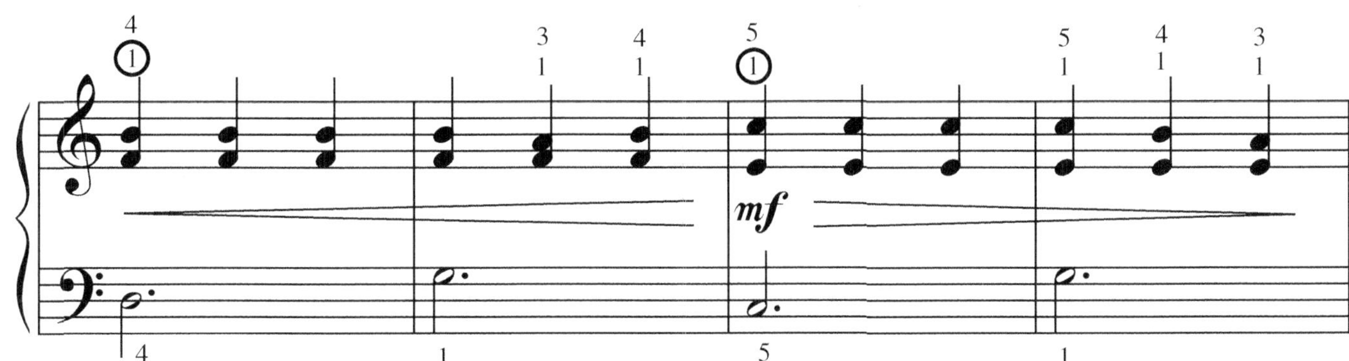

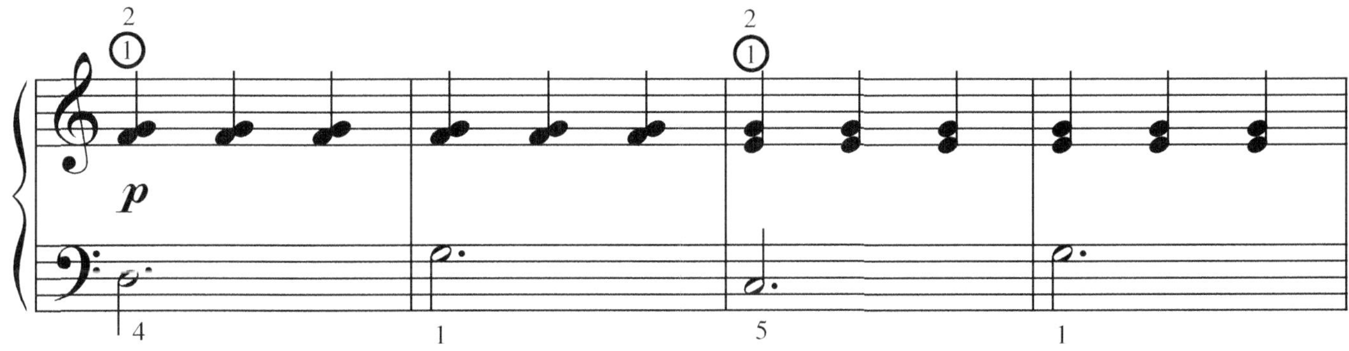

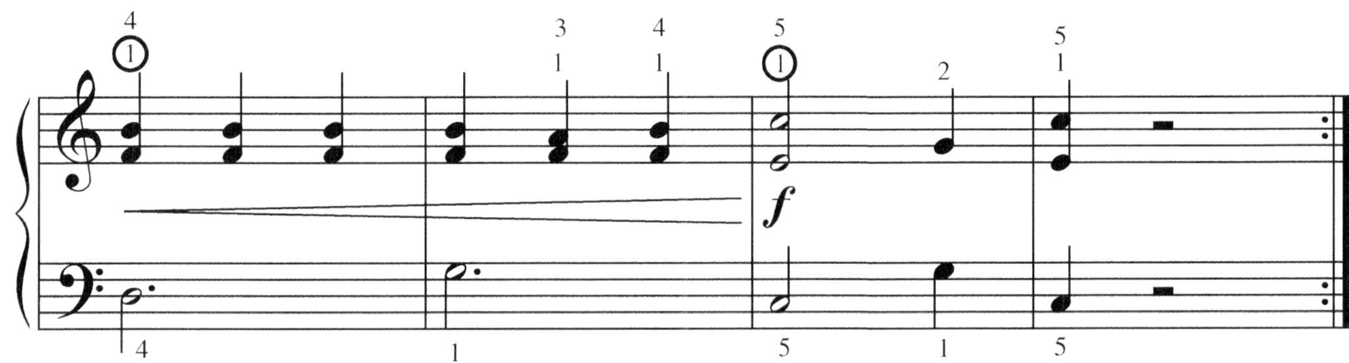

Level 8 pieces

New concepts

1- Chords played with the left hand
2- C major arpeggio played with the right hand
3- Eighth note rests (quaver rests) and dotted quarter rests (dotted crotchet rests)

Changes of position will no longer be indicated by a circle.
See Appendix 2.1 and 2.2 (page 82-83) for chord structure.

C major chord (C)

G7 chord with B as the bass (G7/B)

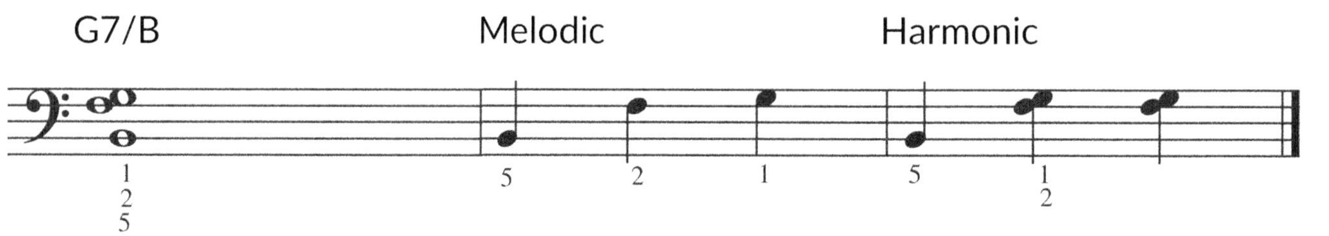

F major chord with C as the bass (F/C)

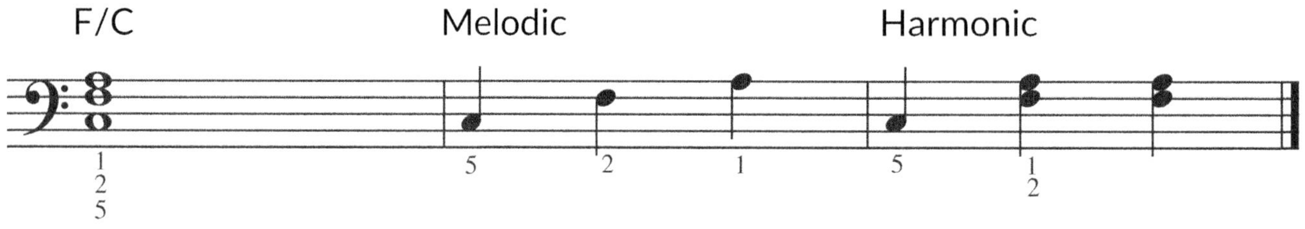

Polly Wolly Doodle

United States (1880)

Dan Emmett
(1815-1904)
Arr. Bobby Cyr

♩ = 120

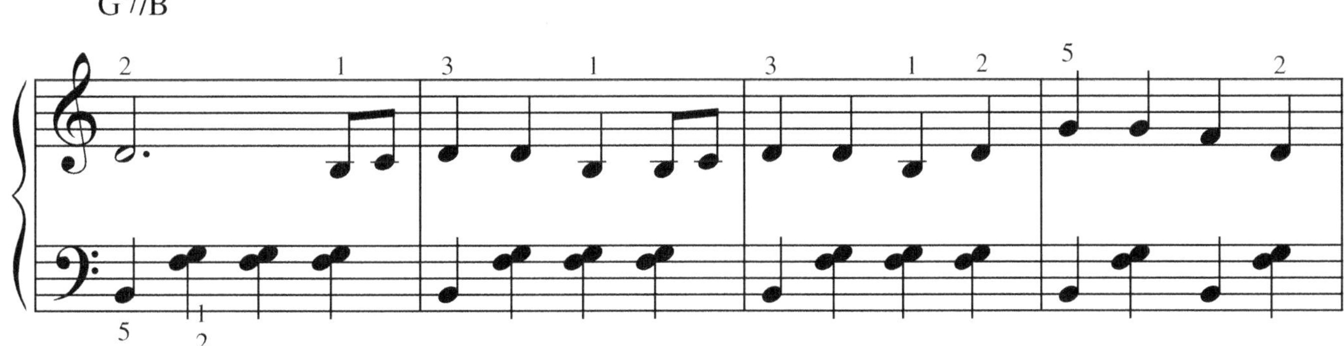

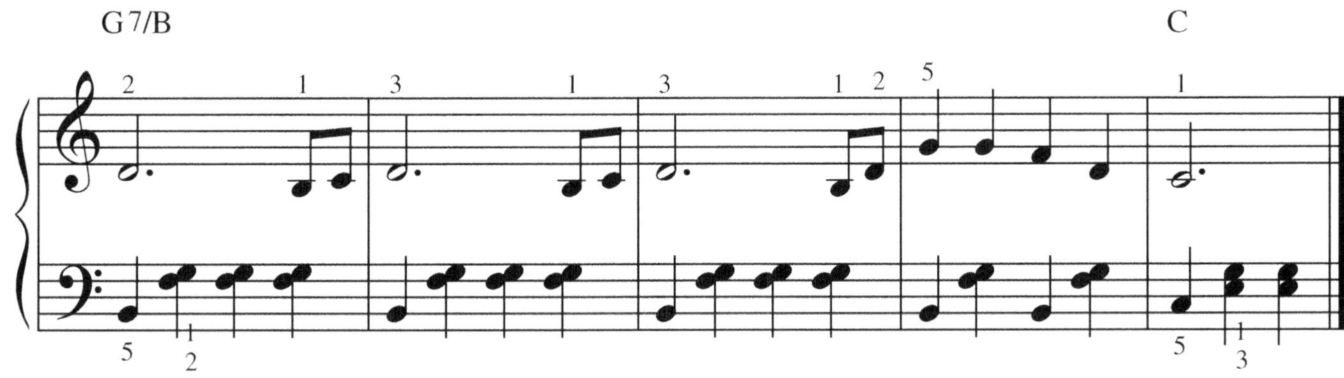

Carnival of Venice

Il carnevale di venezia
Italy (1805)

Niccolo Paganini
(1782-1840)
Arr. Bobby Cyr

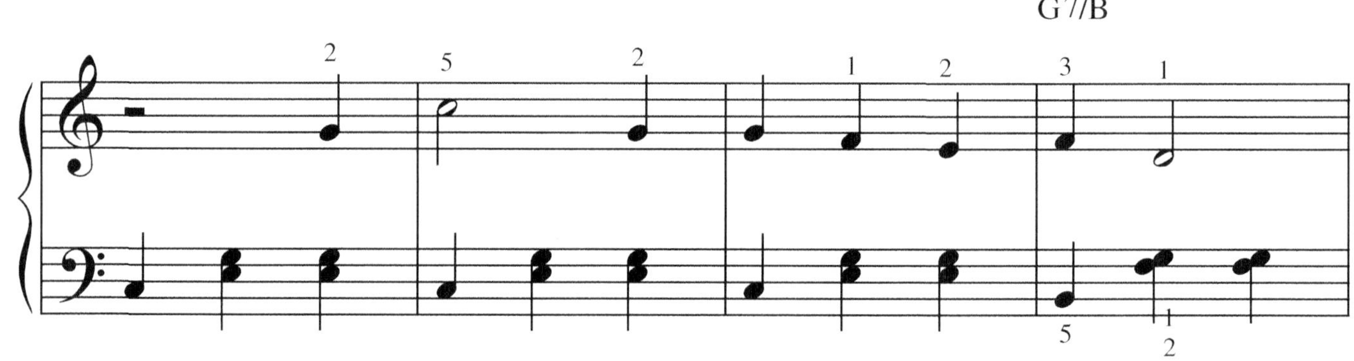

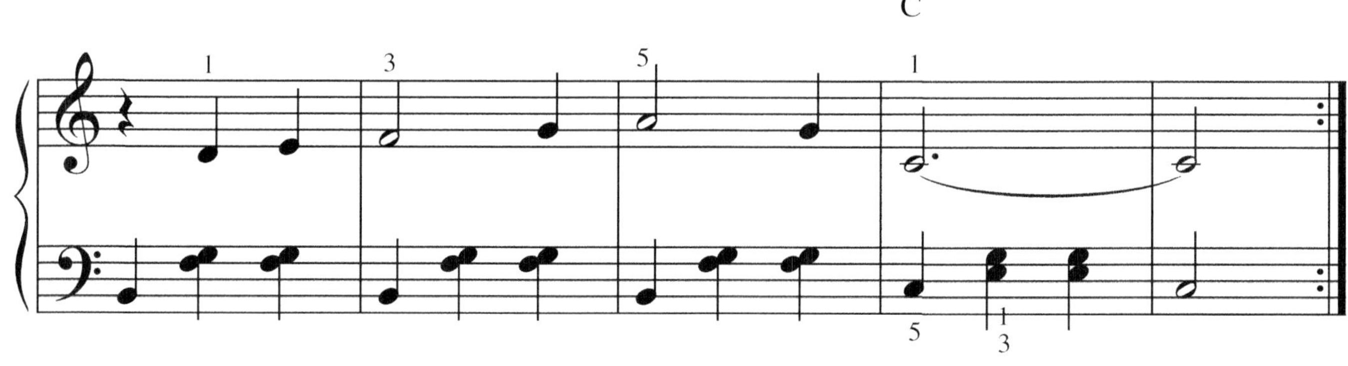

Pretty Little Dutch Girl

United States (1940)

Unknown composer
Roud 12986
Arr. Bobby Cyr

Mary Hamilton

Scotland

Unknown composer
Roud 79
Arr. Bobby Cyr

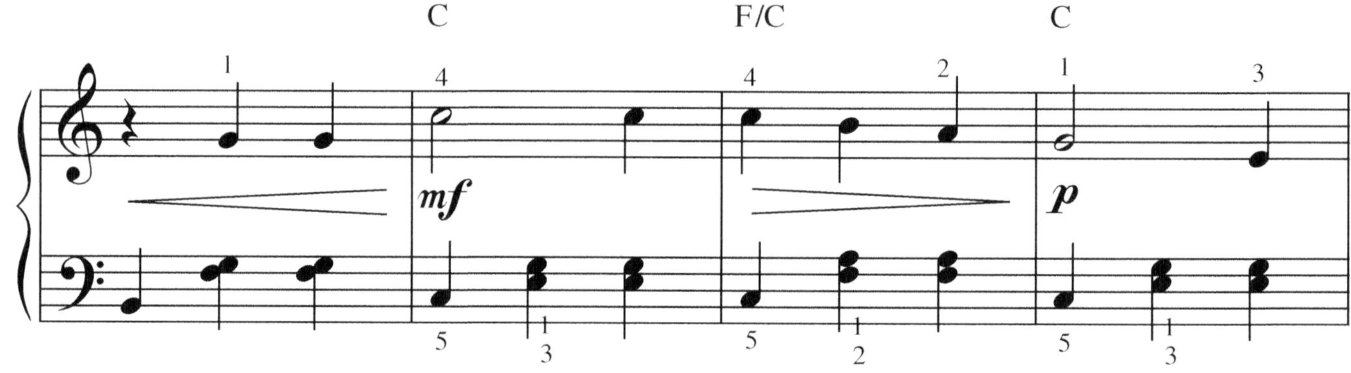

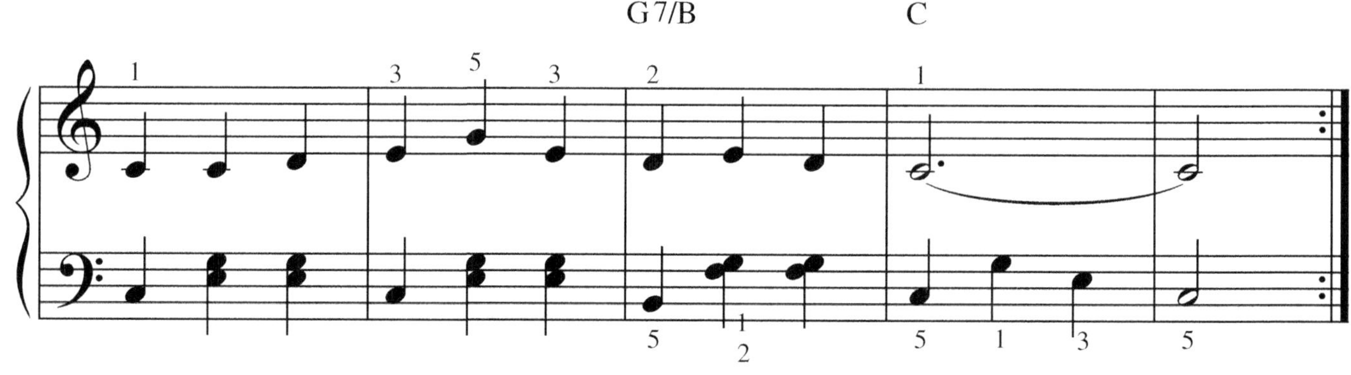

Jesus Loves Me

United States (1862)

William Batchelder Bradbury
(1816-1868)
Arr. Bobby Cyr

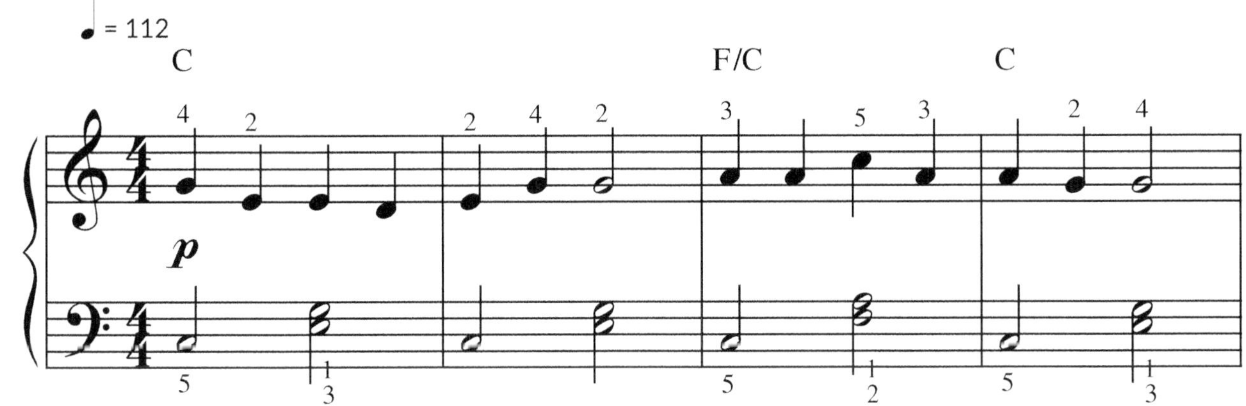

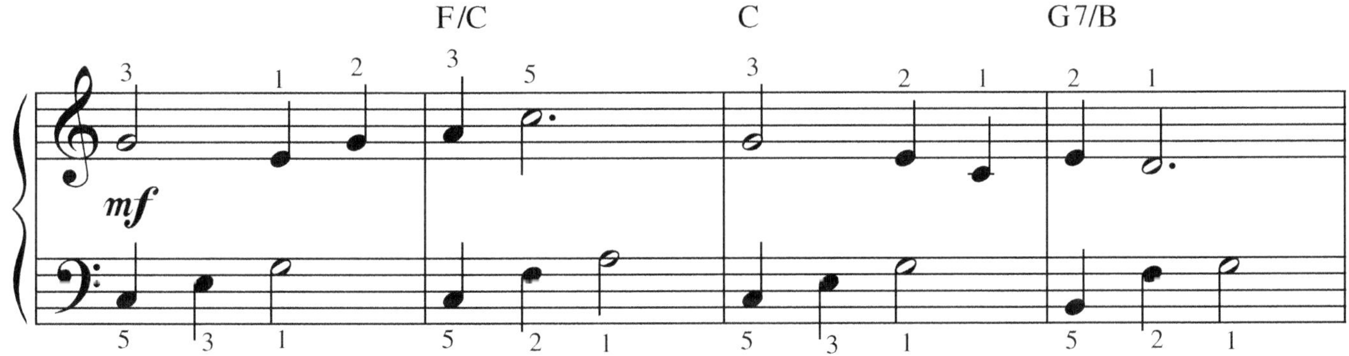

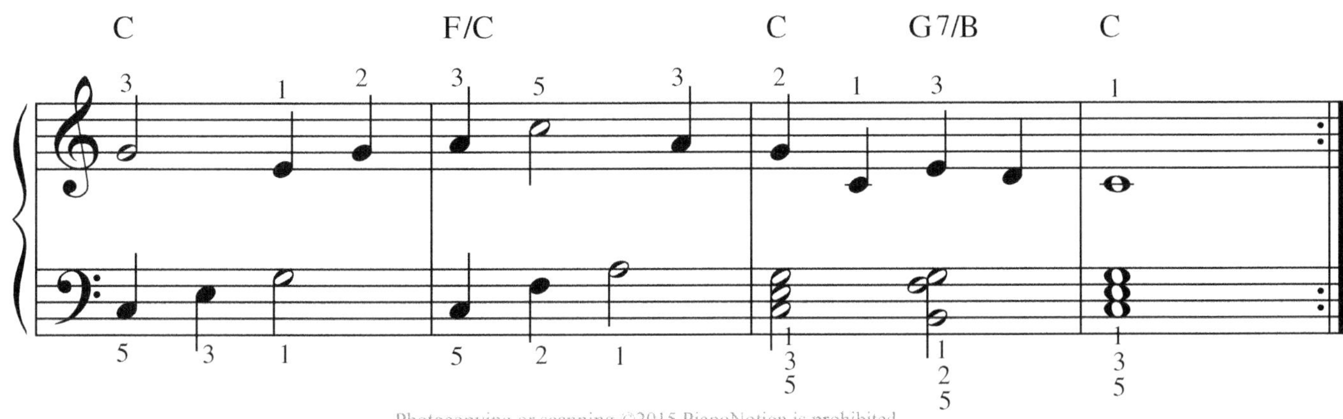

C major arpeggio – right hand

An arpeggio is a broken chord: the notes are played one after the other rather than simultaneously. An arpeggio may span more than one octave.

Exercise: Play the C arpeggio with your right hand.

Camptown Races

United States (1850)

Stephen Foster
(1826-1864)
Arr. Bobby Cyr

♩ = 112

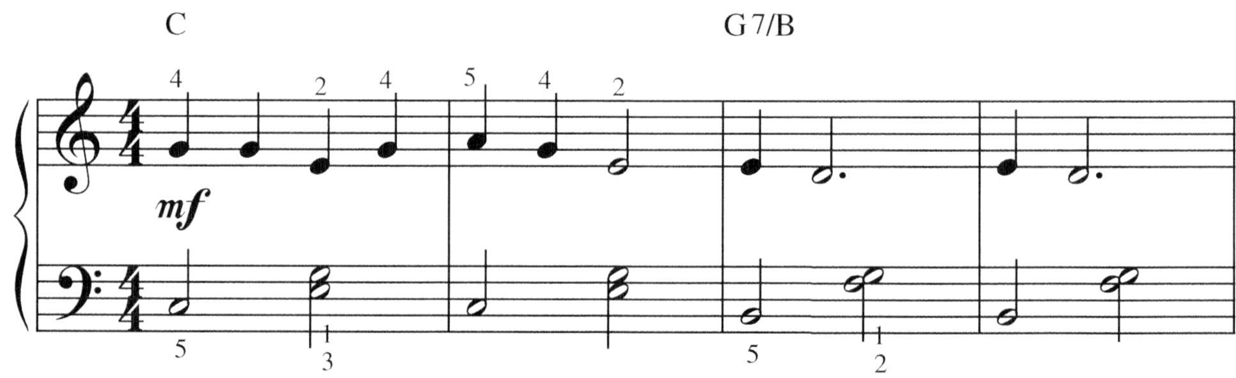

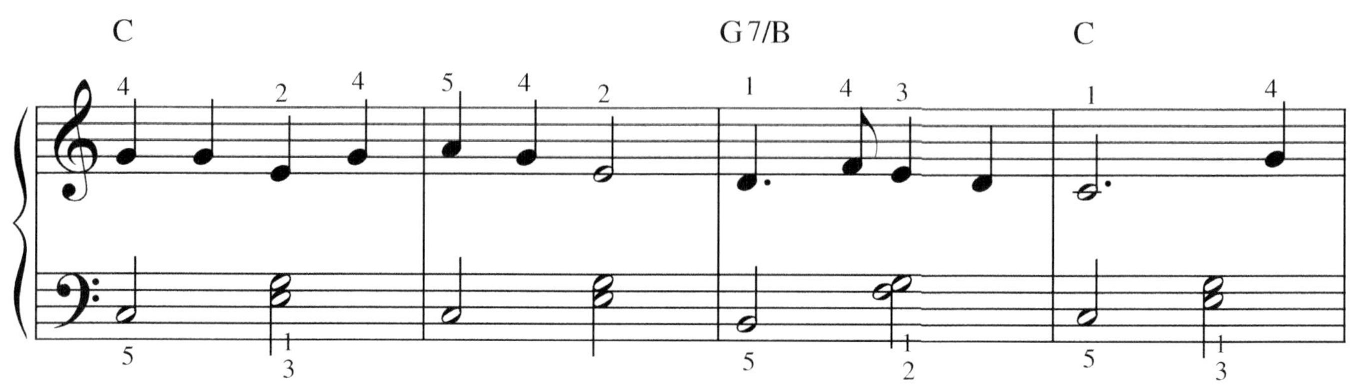

Camptown Races

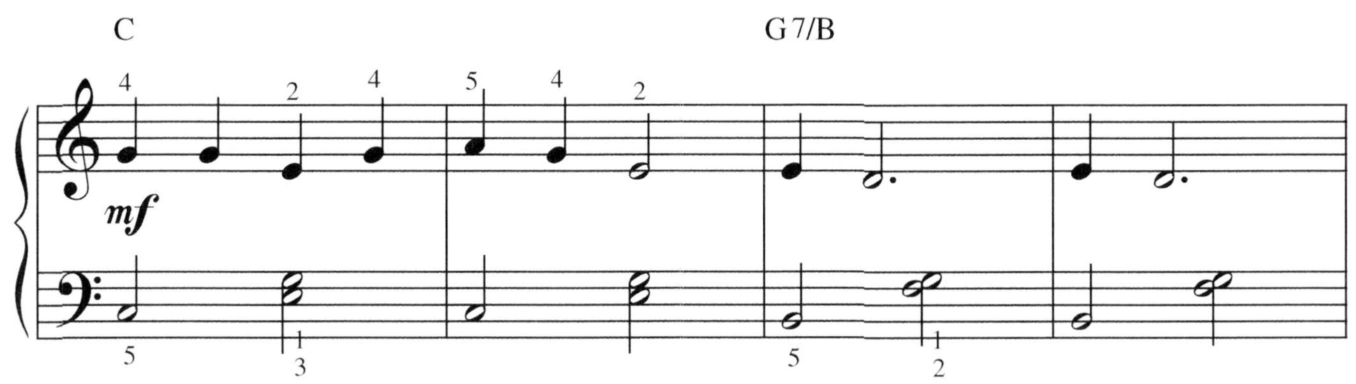

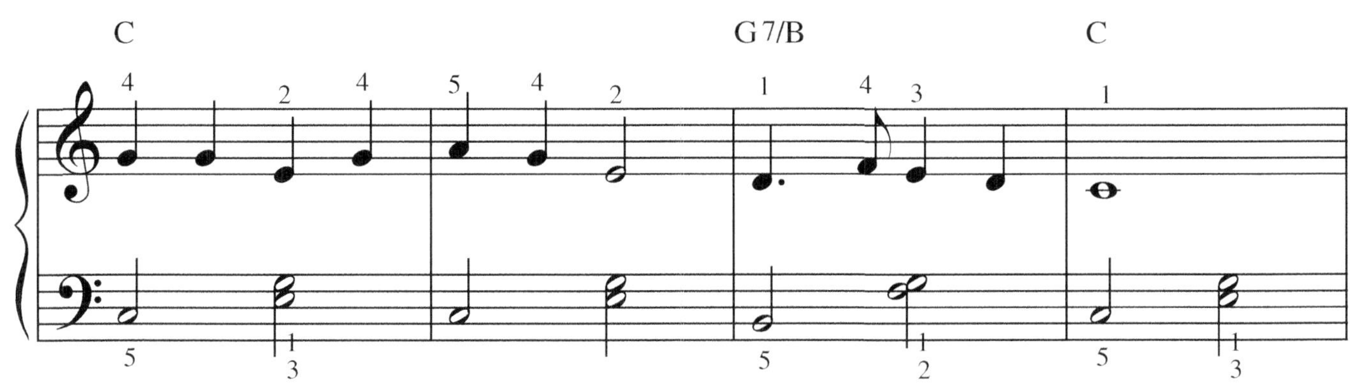

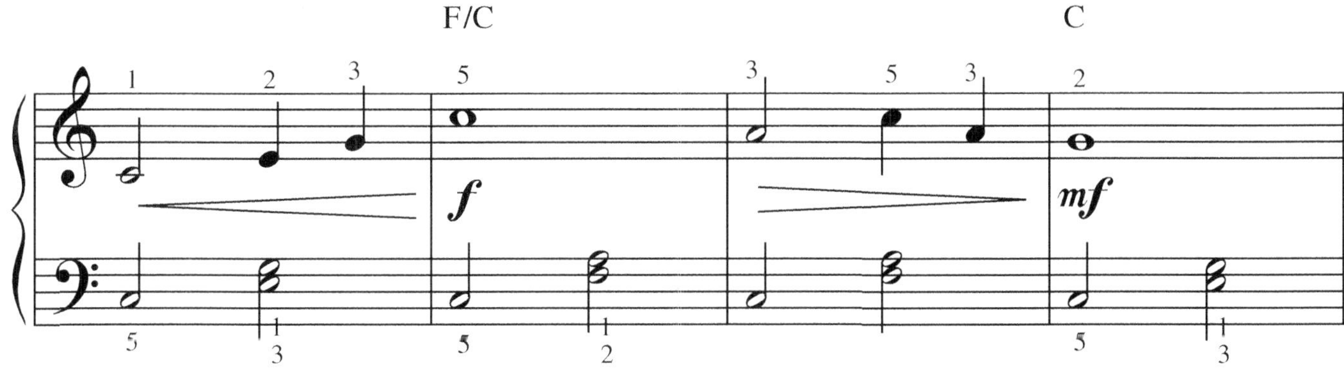

Scotland the Brave

Scotland (1895)

Unknown composer
Arr. Bobby Cyr

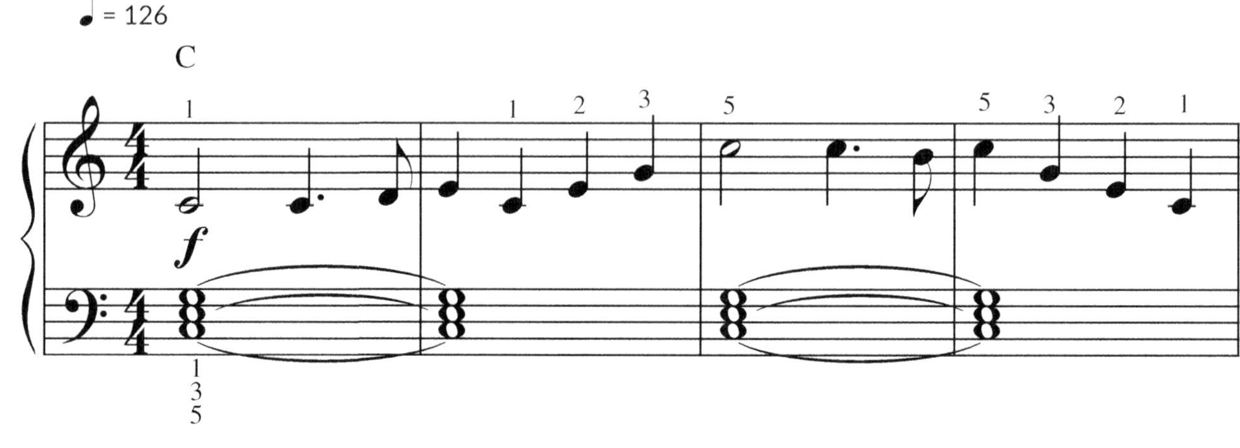

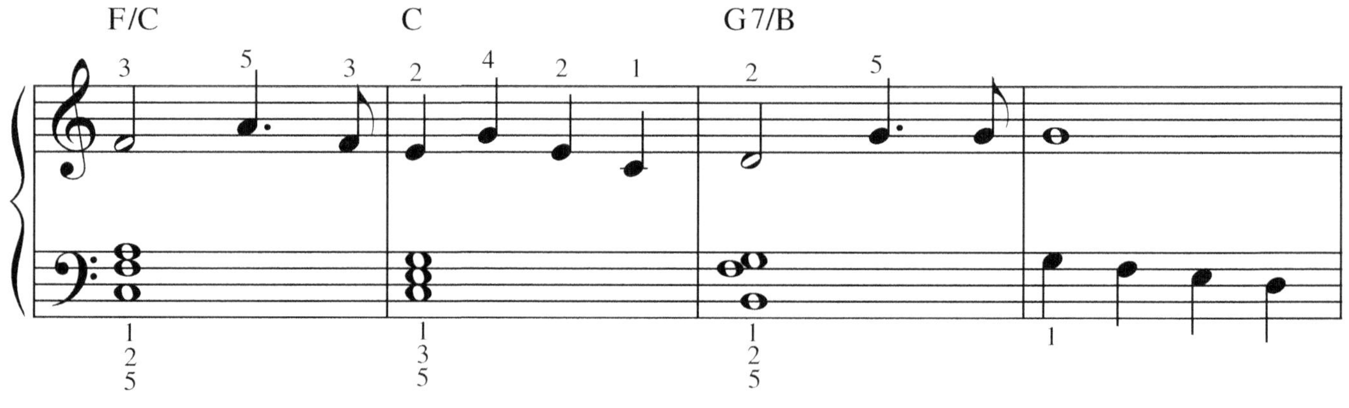

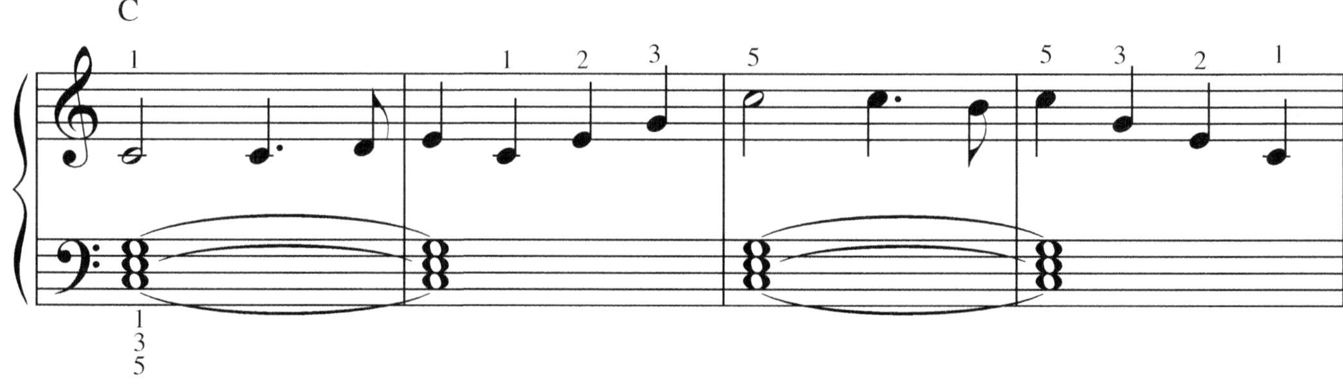

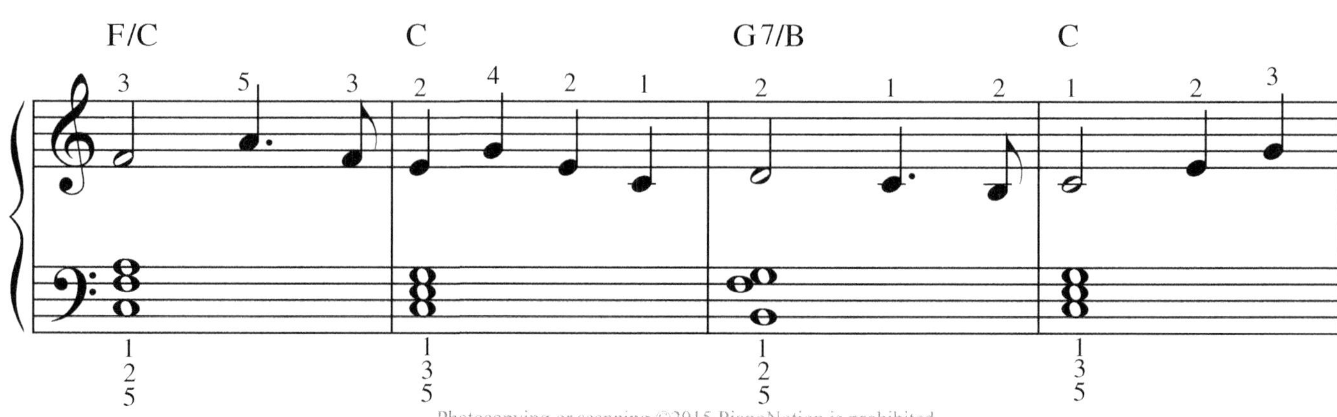

Scotland the Brave

Eighth note rests | Quaver rests

An eighth note rest is equal to the value of an eighth note. 𝄾 = ♪

Exercise: see Appendix 1.1 (page 79)

Banks of the Ohio

United States (1920)

Unknown composer
Roud 157
Arr. Bobby Cyr

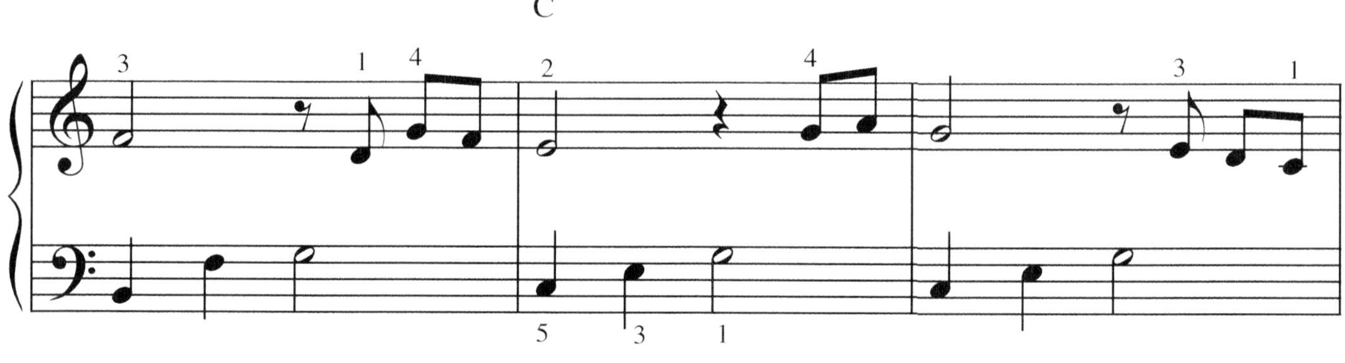

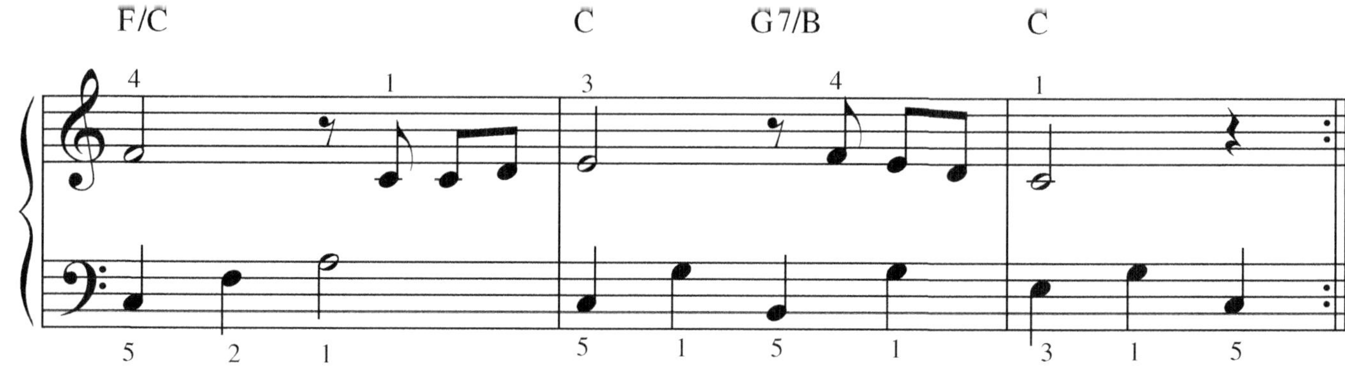

A dotted quarter rest is equal to the value of a dotted quarter note. 𝄽. = ♩.

He's Got the Whole World in His Hands

United States (1927)

Unknown composer
Roud 7501
Arr. Bobby Cyr

Minor chord

In a minor chord, the third is one half step lower than the third of the major chord.
Examples: C major is played (C, E, G) and C minor is played (C, E♭, G).
D major is played (D, F♯, A) and D minor is played (D, F, A).

D minor chord (Dm)

Ievan Polkka

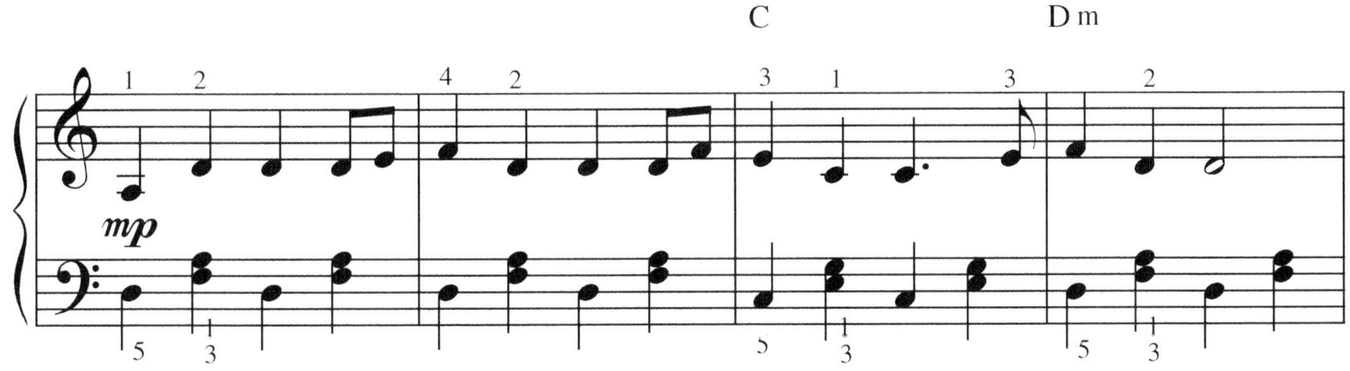

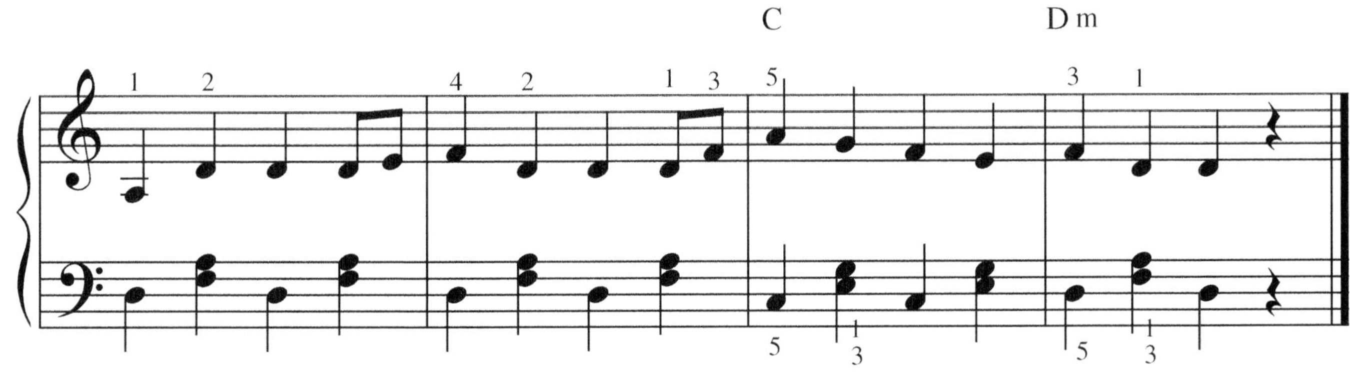

Drunken Sailor

Ireland (1869)

Unknown composer
Roud 322
Arr. Bobby Cyr

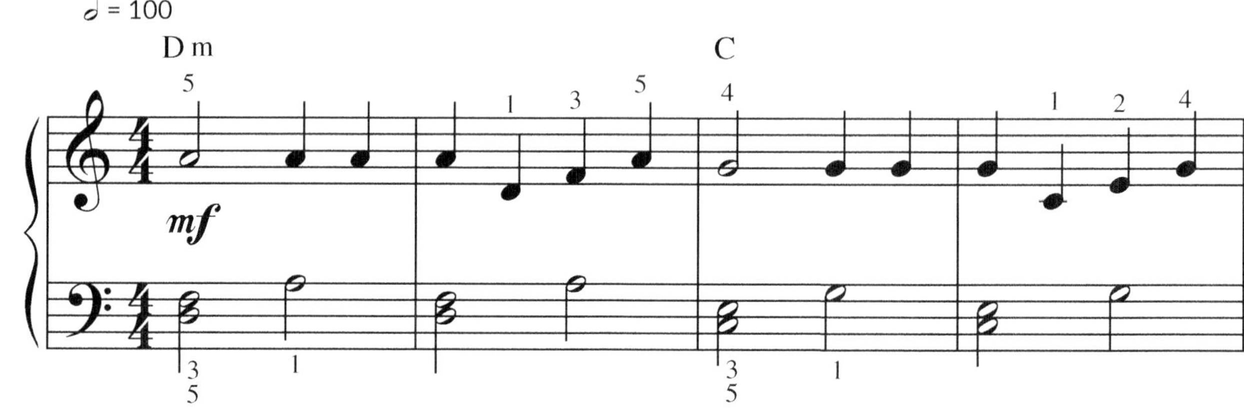

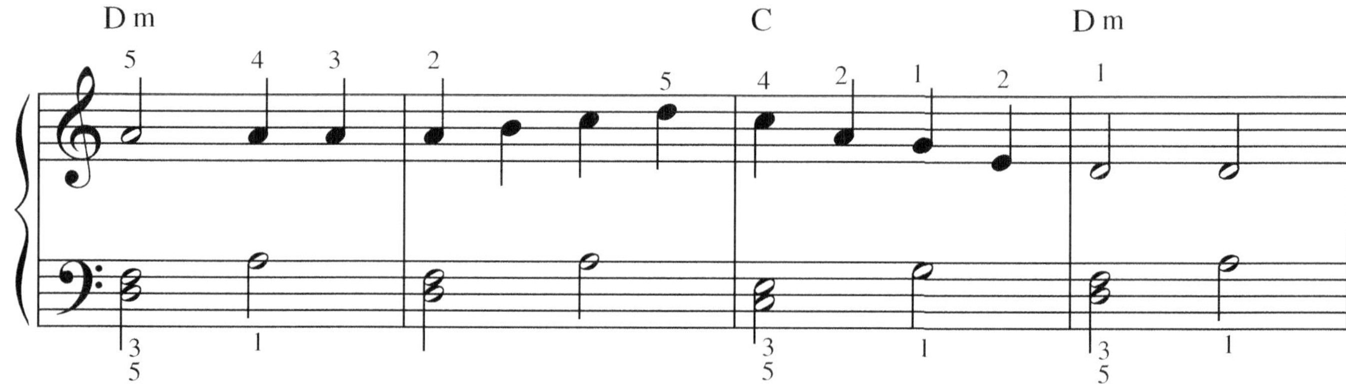

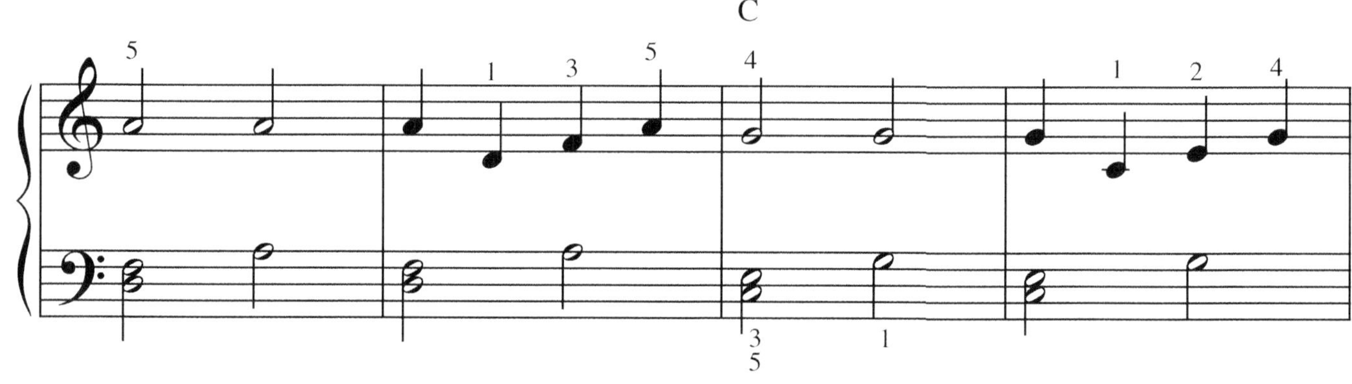

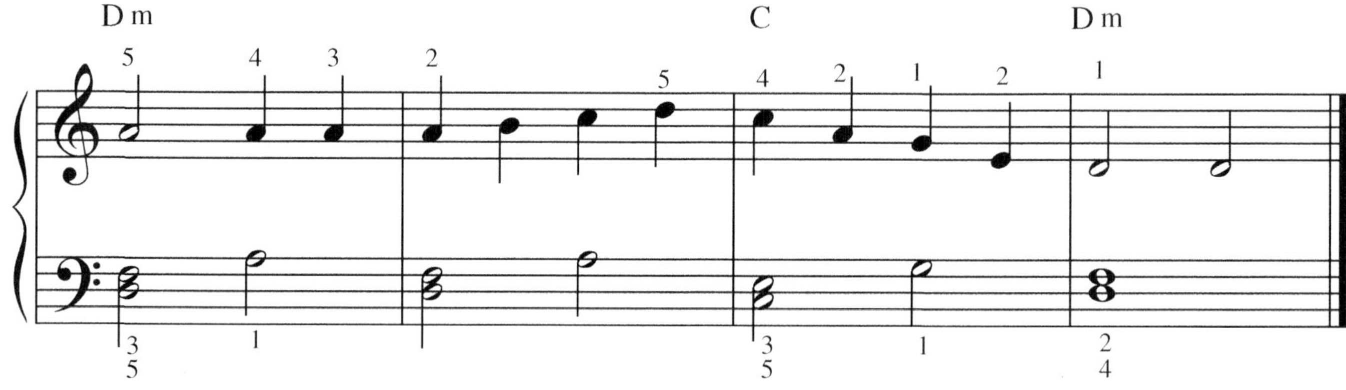

Scarborough Fair

The Elfin Knight
England

Unknown composer
Roud 12
Arr. Bobby Cyr

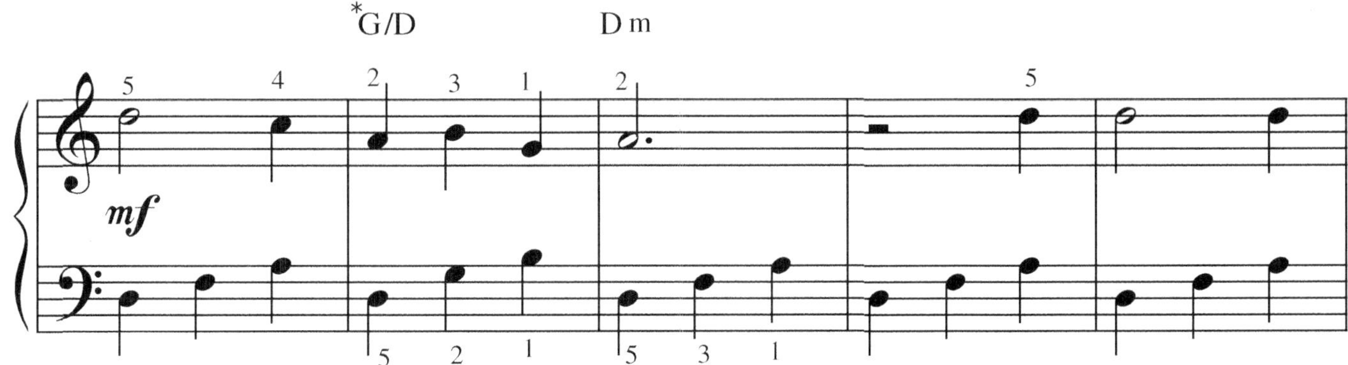

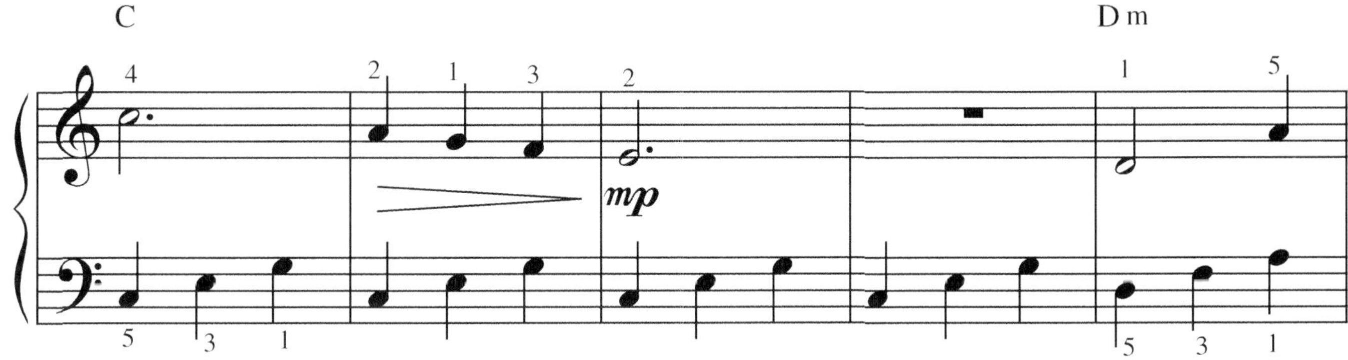

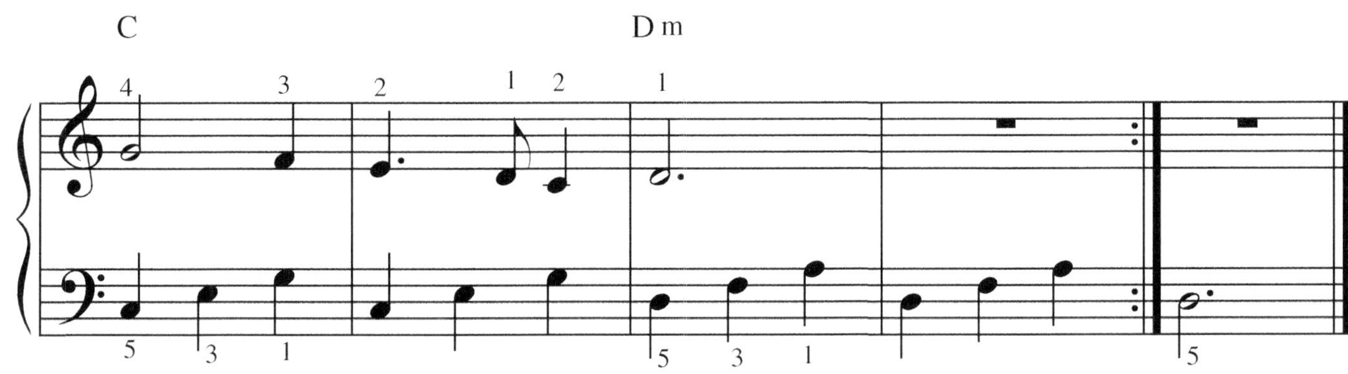

* See the G/D chord details on page 68

Level 9 pieces

The 6/8 time signature

In 6/8, the eighth note represents one beat.
A quarter note is equal to 2 beats, and a dotted quarter note is equal to 3 beats.
There are 6 beats per measure, grouped into 2 groups of 3 eighth notes.

Example:

Exercise: see Appendix 1.2 (page 80)

I Saw Three Ships

Come Sailing In
England (1833)

Unknown composer
Roud 700
Arr. Bobby Cyr

I Saw Three Ships

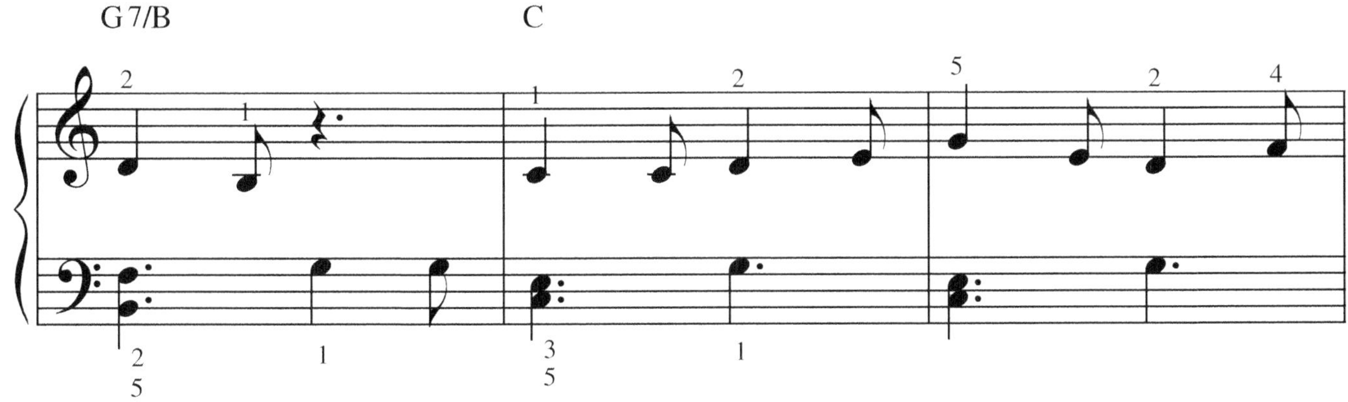

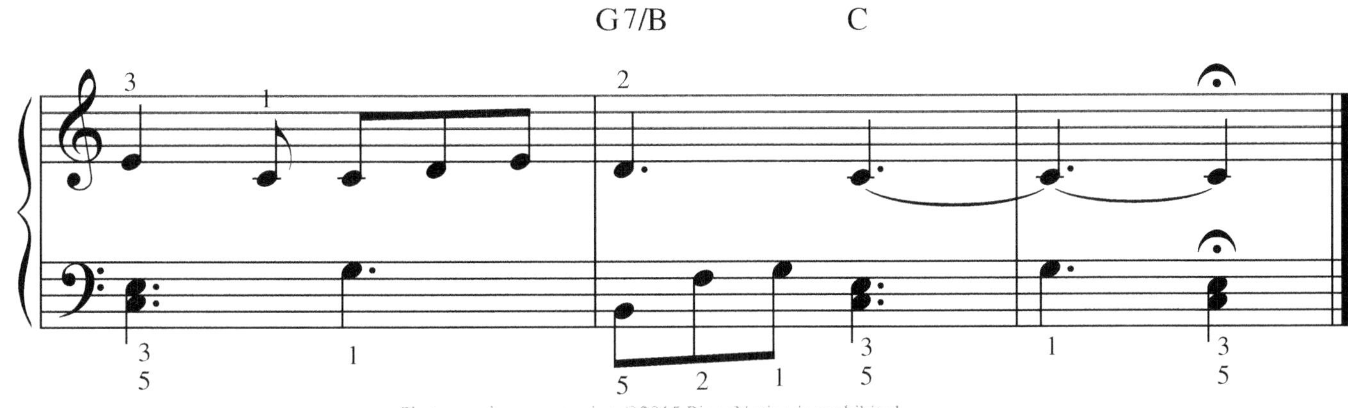

Three Blind Mice

England (1805)

Unknown composer
Roud 3753
Arr. Bobby Cyr

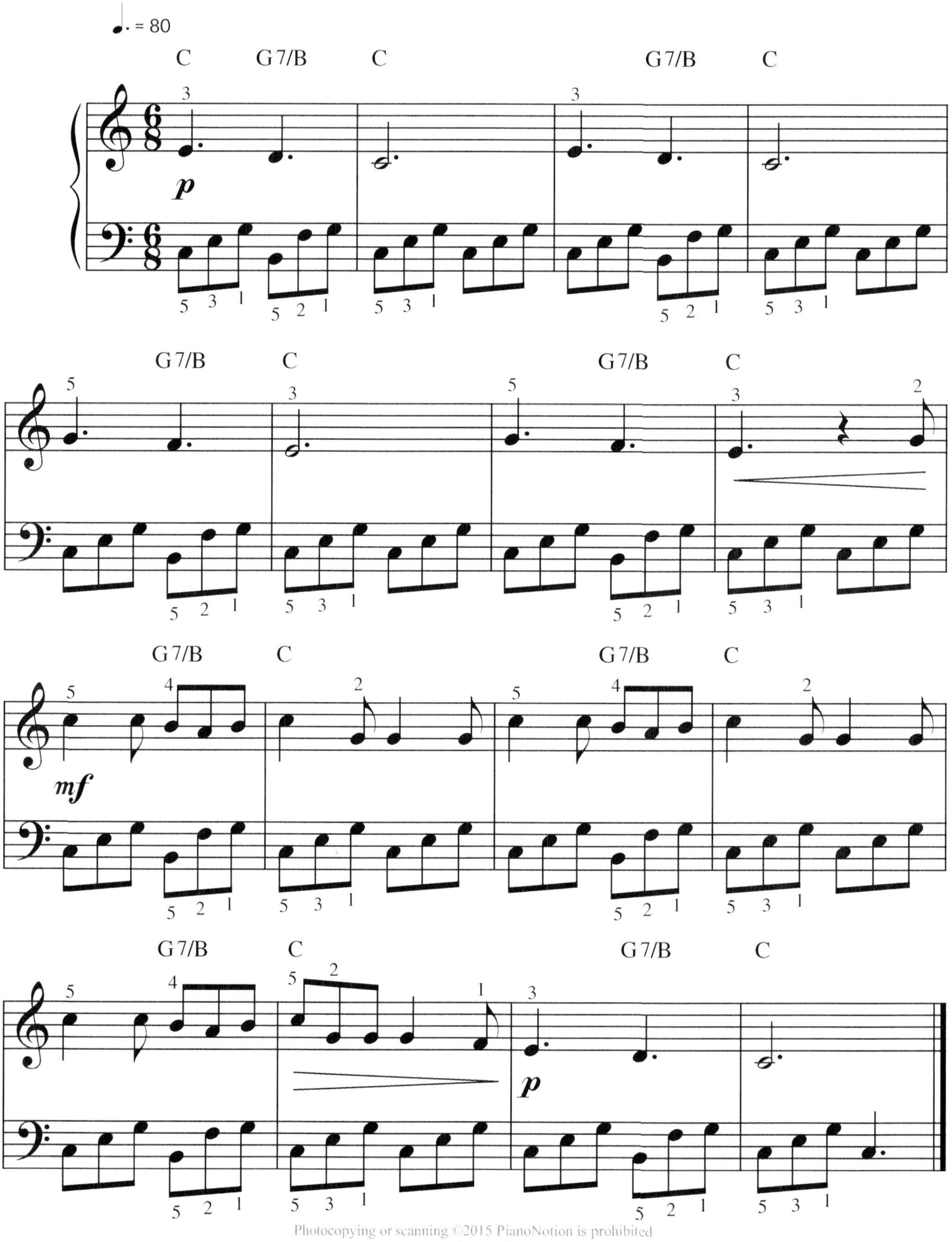

♩. = 80

C G7/B C G7/B C

G7/B C G7/B C

G7/B C G7/B C

G7/B C G7/B C

Brian Boru's March

Ireland (1014)

Unknown composer
Arr. Bobby Cyr

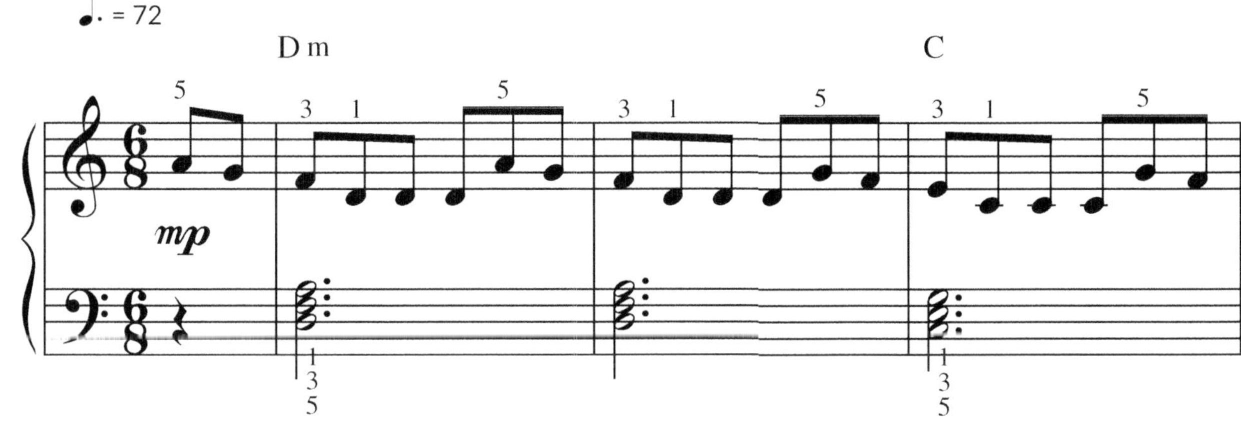

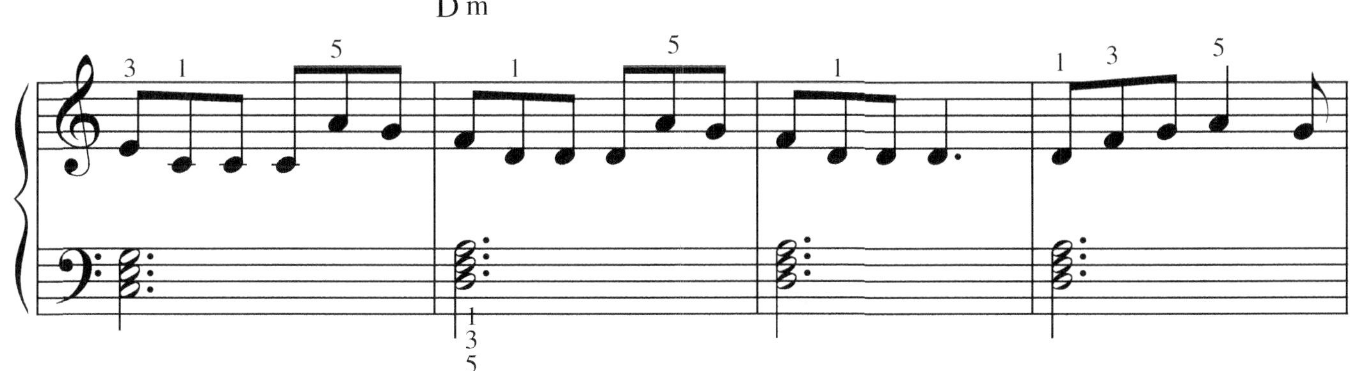

G major chord with B as the bass (G/B)

G/B
Melodic
Harmonic

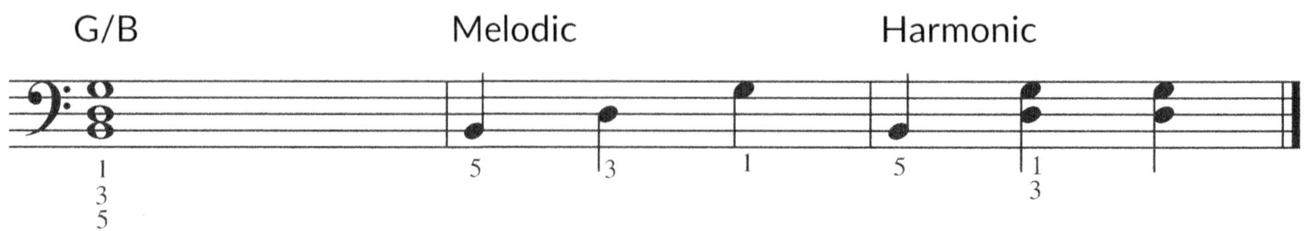

Do not confuse G/B with G7/B.

Review: G7 chord with B as the bass (G7/B)

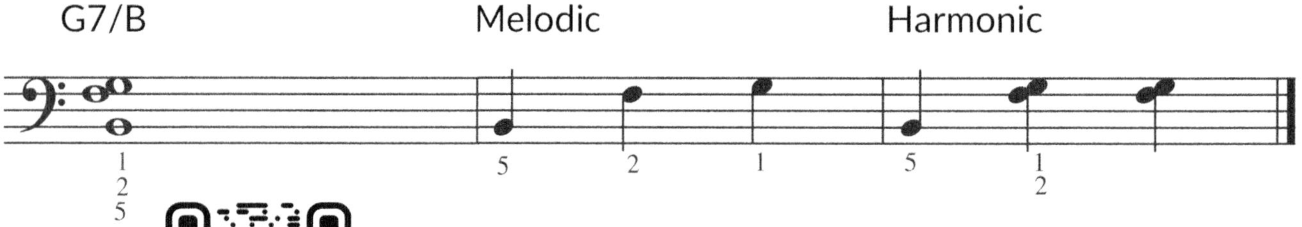

G7/B
Melodic
Harmonic

La Raspa

Mexico

Unknown composer
Arr. Bobby Cyr

♩. = 80
C
mf
G/B
C

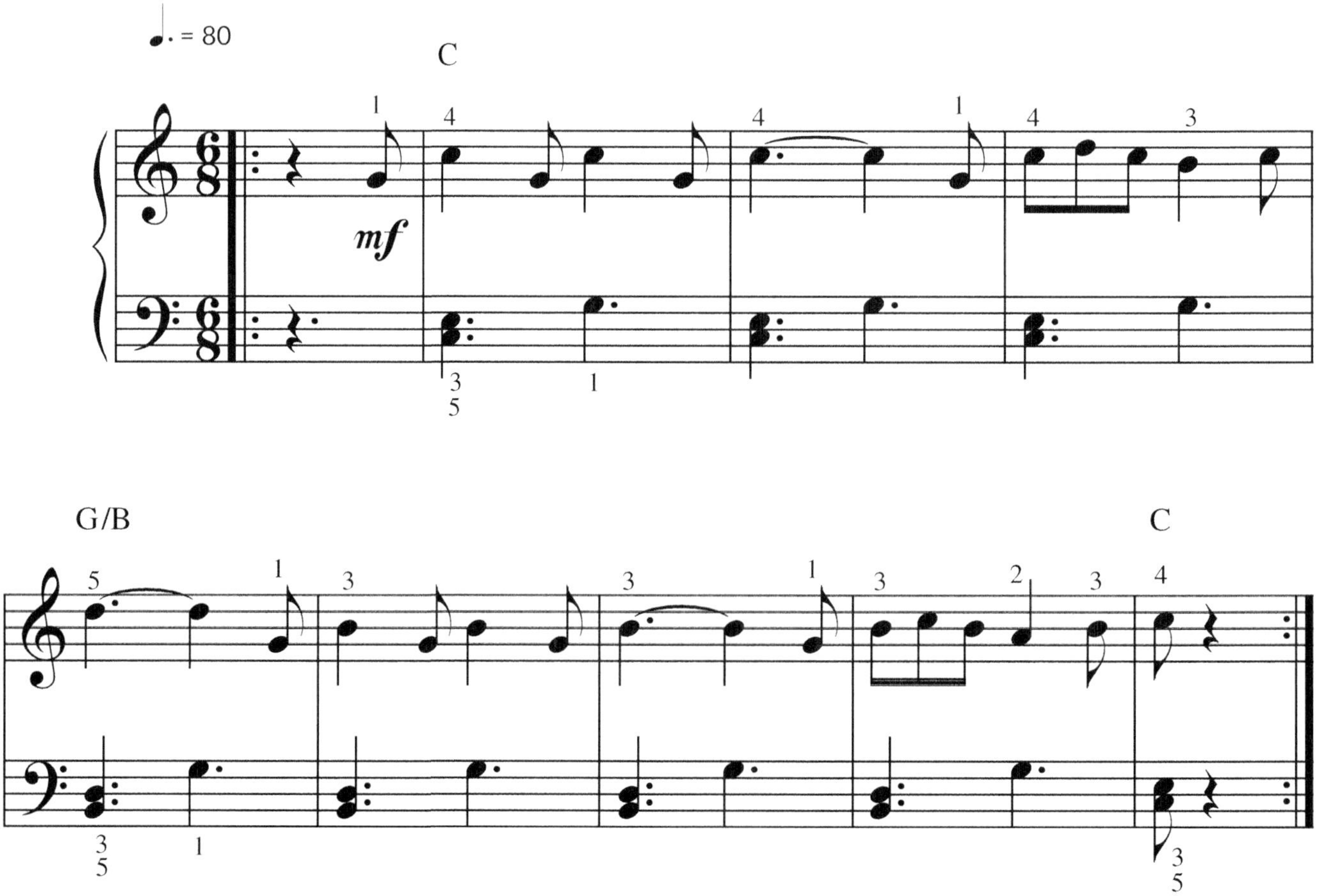

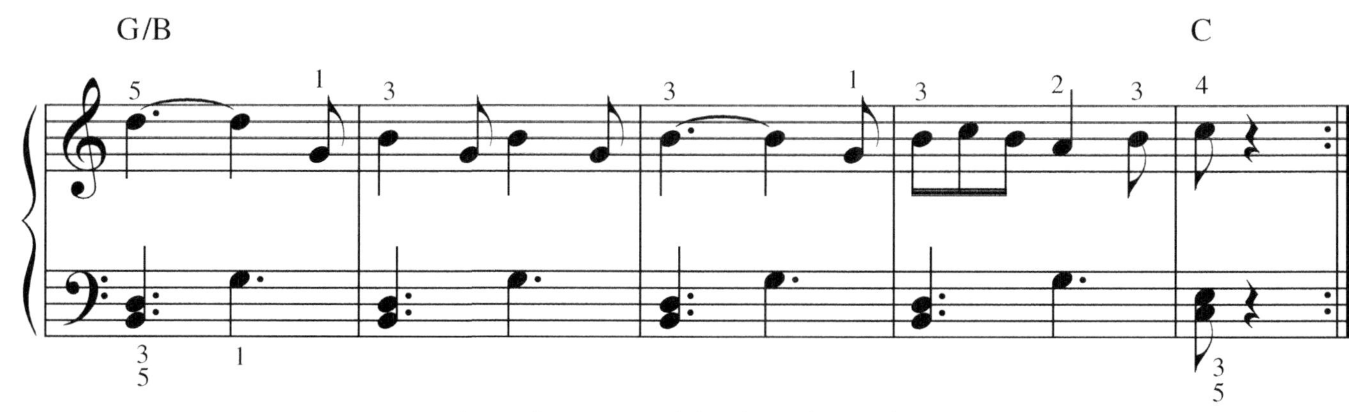

La Raspa

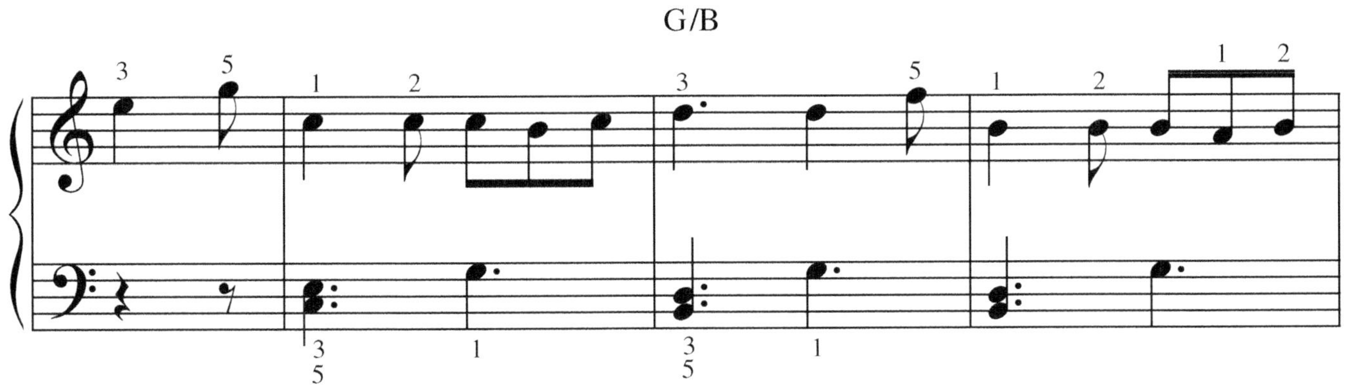

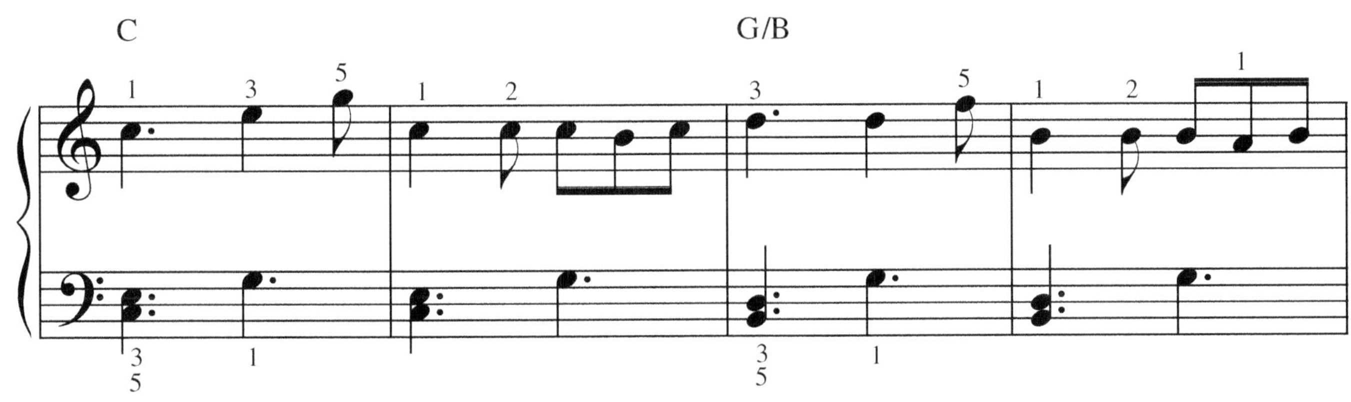

F major chord (F)

F | Melodic | Harmonic

1
3
5
5 3 1
5 1
3

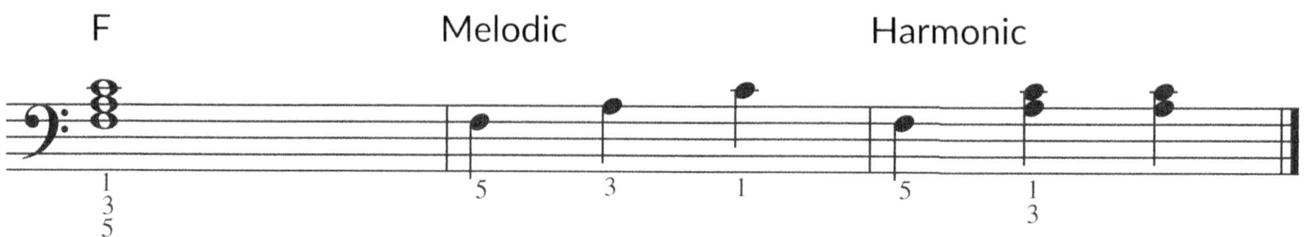

C major chord with E as the bass (C/E)

C/E | Melodic | Harmonic

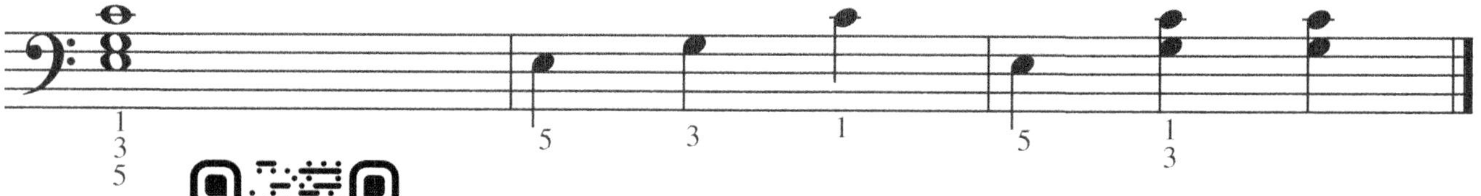

1
3
5
5 3 1
5 1
3

Silent Night

Austria (1818)

Franz Xaver Gruber
(1787-1863)
Arr. Bobby Cyr

♩ = 120

C
3
1
3
1
mp
5
3

G/B
C
5
3
4
1
5
1
3
5
1
3

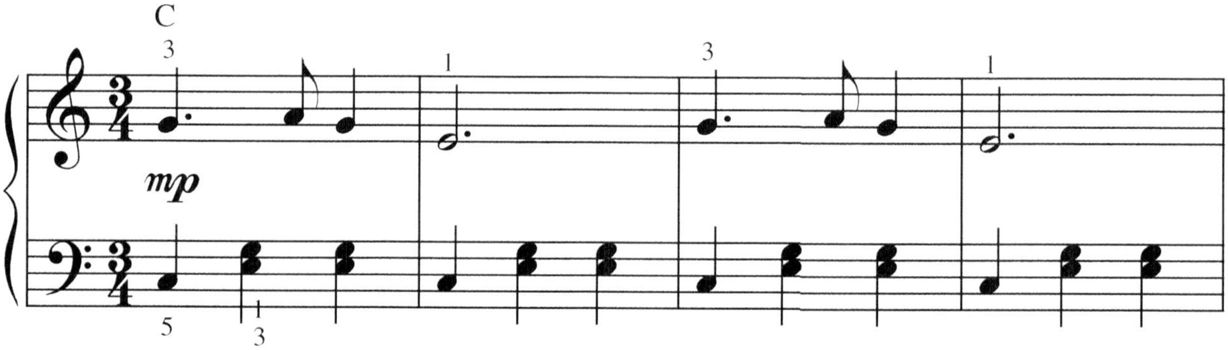

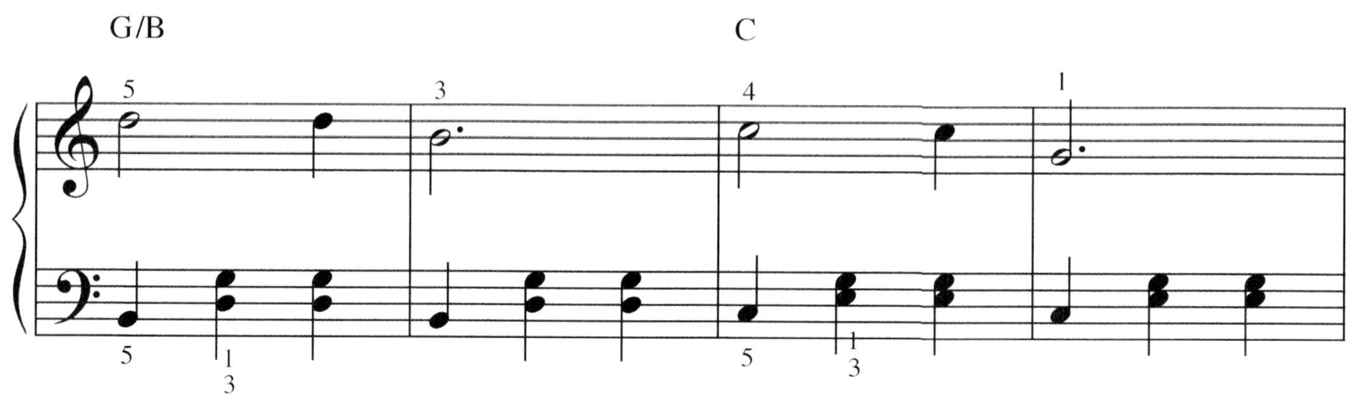

Silent Night

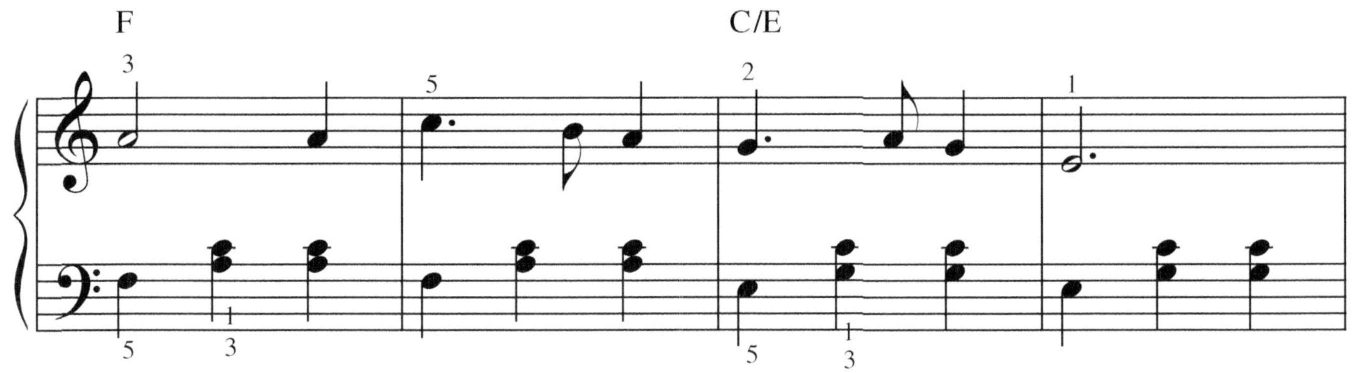

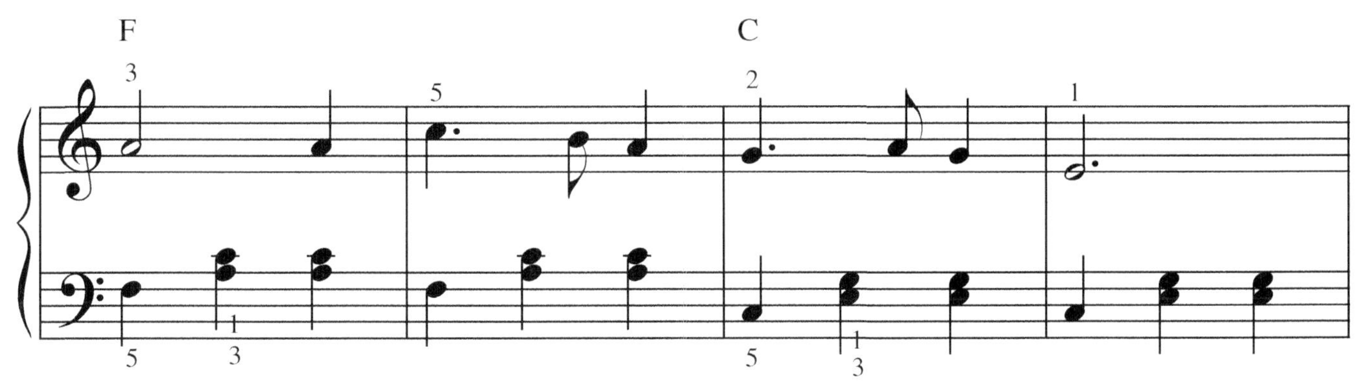

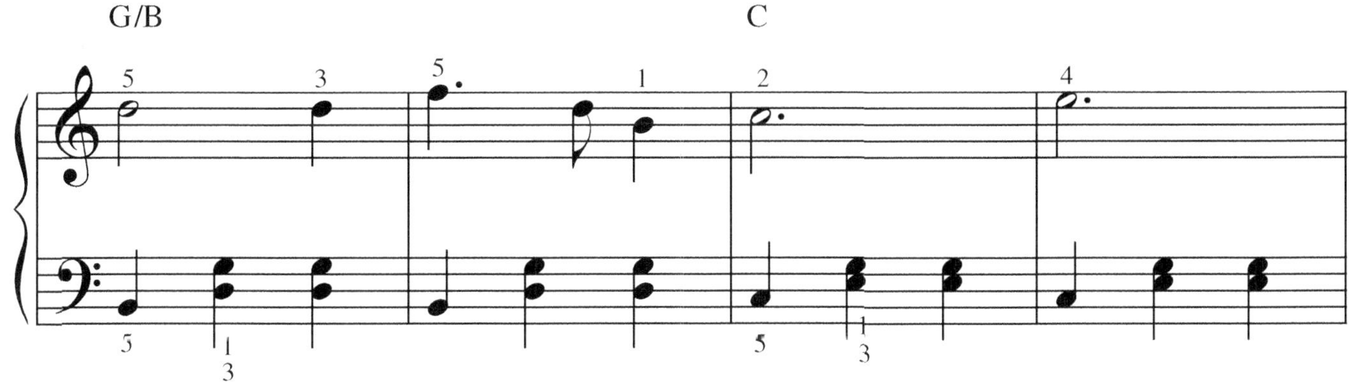

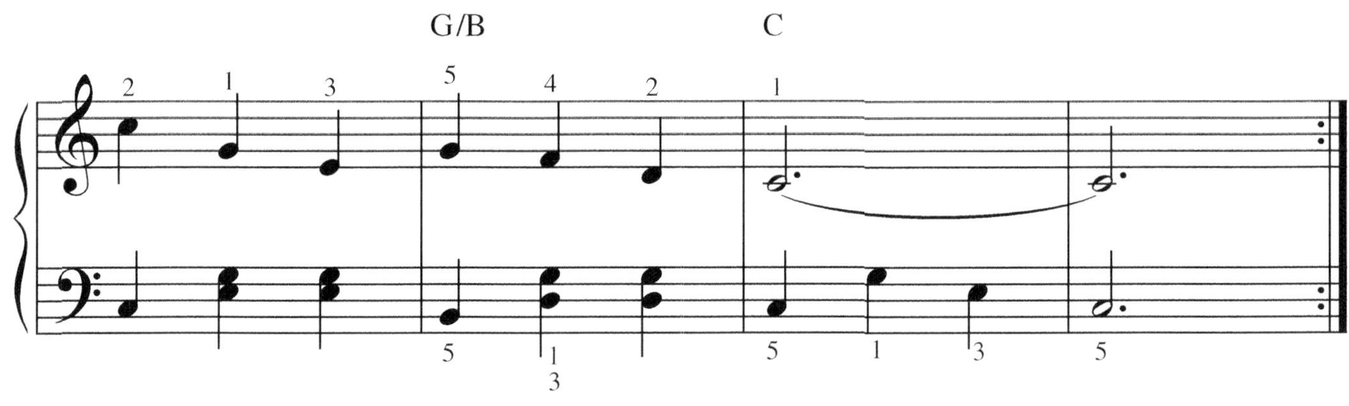

Botany Bay

England (1855)

Wilhelm Meyer Lutz
(1829–1903)
Arr. Bobby Cyr

♩ = 108

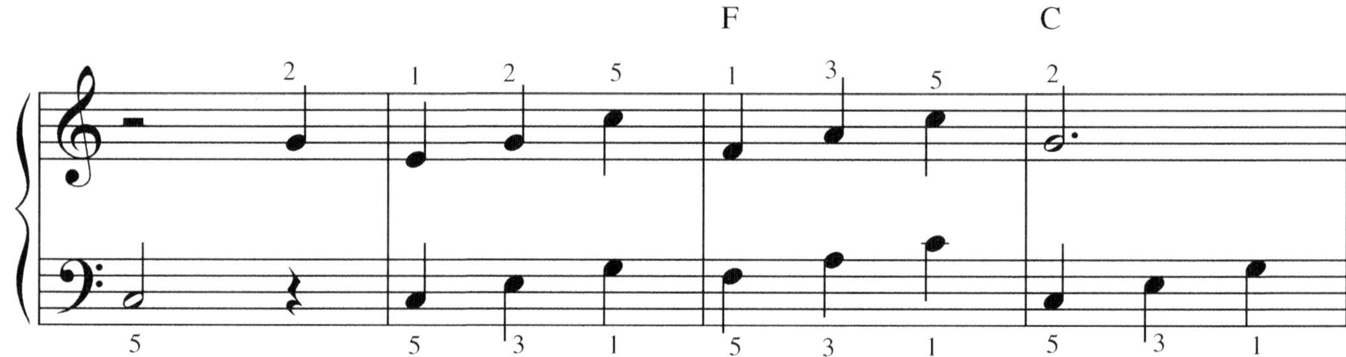

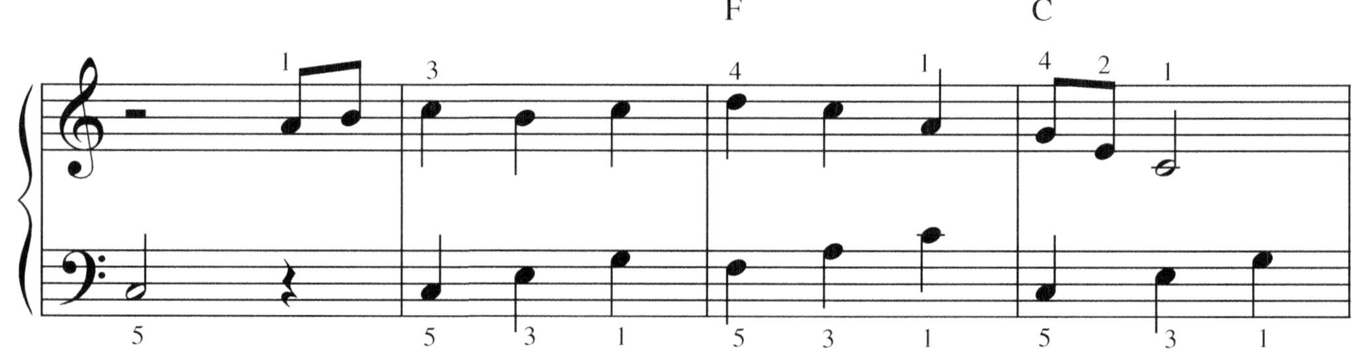

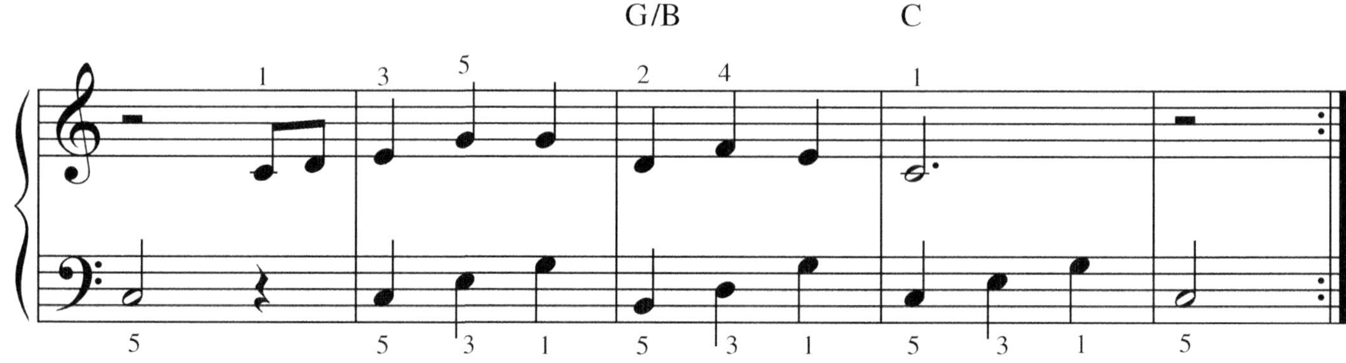

The Marines' Hymn

Gendarmes Duet
France (1867)

Jacques Offenbach
(1819-1880)
Arr. Bobby Cyr

♩ = 112

C G/B C G/B
C G/B C G/B
C F C/E F
C/E C G/B C G/B C

Chiapanecas

Mexico

Bulmaro López Fernández
(1878–1960)
Arr. Bobby Cyr

Chiapanecas

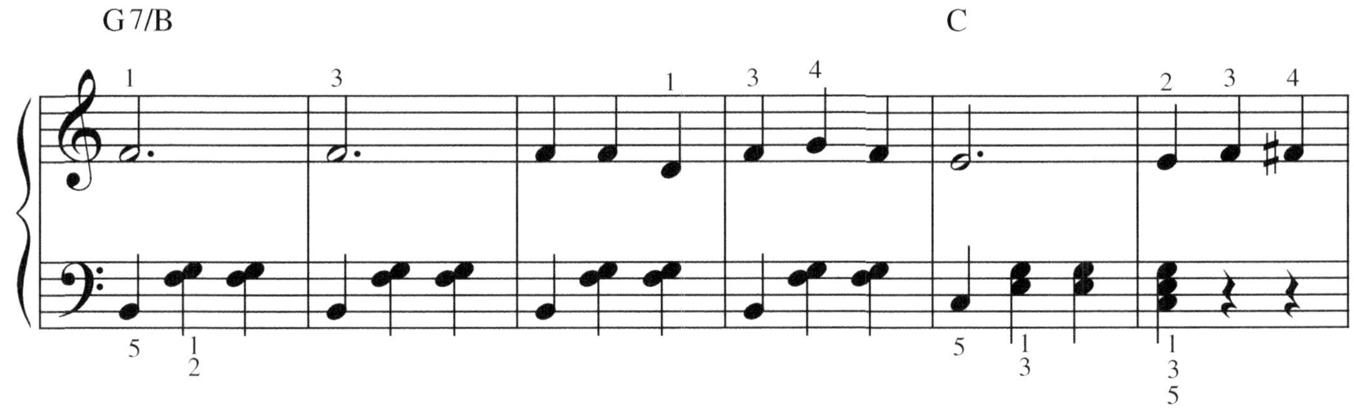

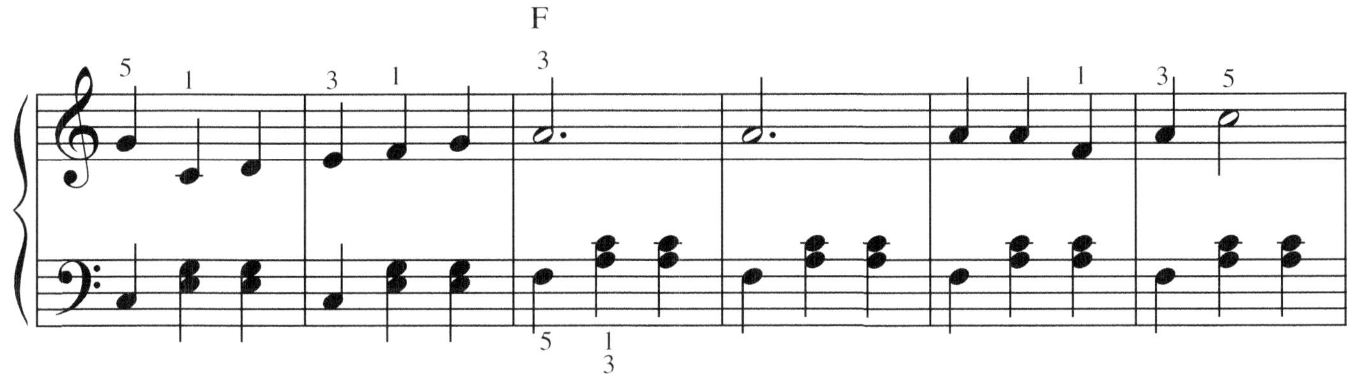

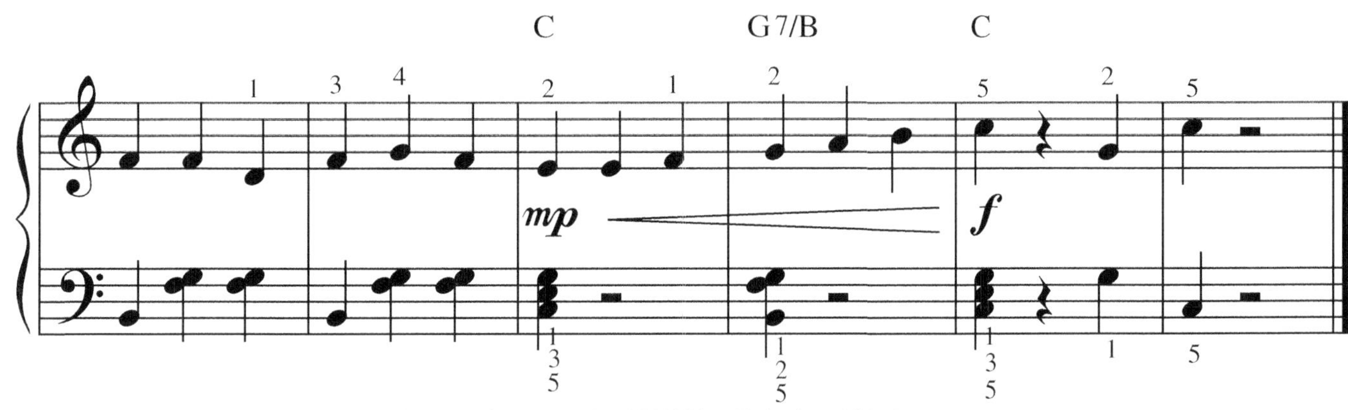

Level 10 pieces

F major

A key signature with one flat (B flat) indicates that the piece is in F Major.
To better understand the key of F major, play the F scale and take note of the B flat.

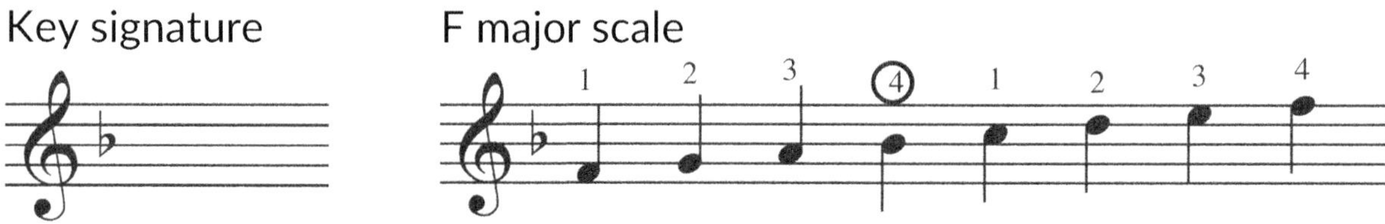

F major chord (F)

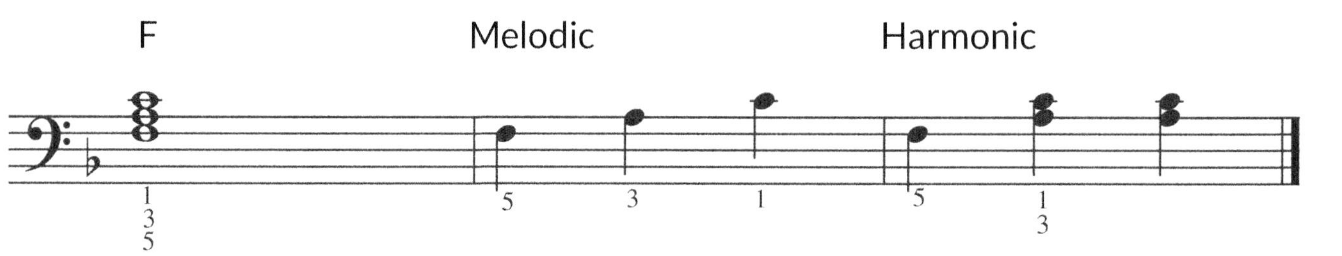

C7 chord with E as the bass (C7/E)

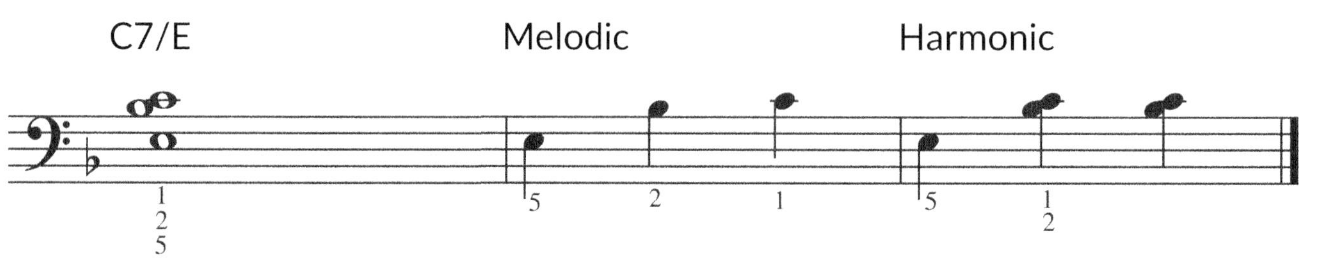

Bb major chord with F as the bass (Bb/F)

Mary Ann

England (1930)

Unknown composer
Roud 4438
Arr. Bobby Cyr

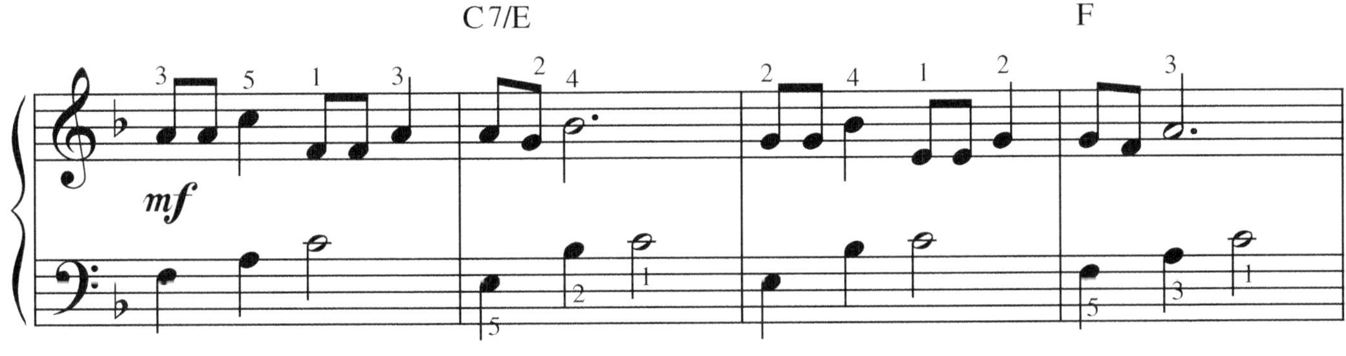

A Tisket A Tasket

United States (1879)

Unknown composer
Roud 13188
Arr. Bobby Cyr

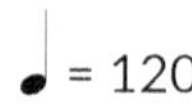

When The World's On Fire

United States (1919)

Unknown composer
Roud 4225
Arr. Bobby Cyr

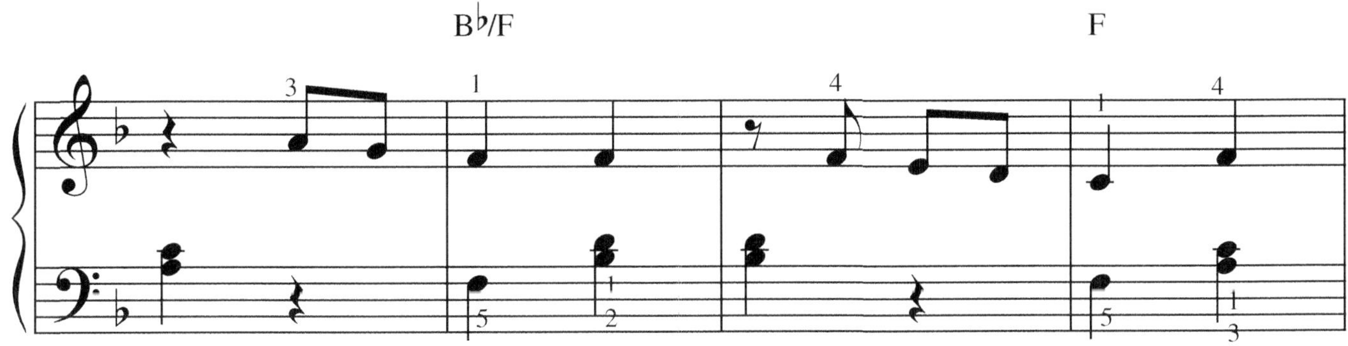

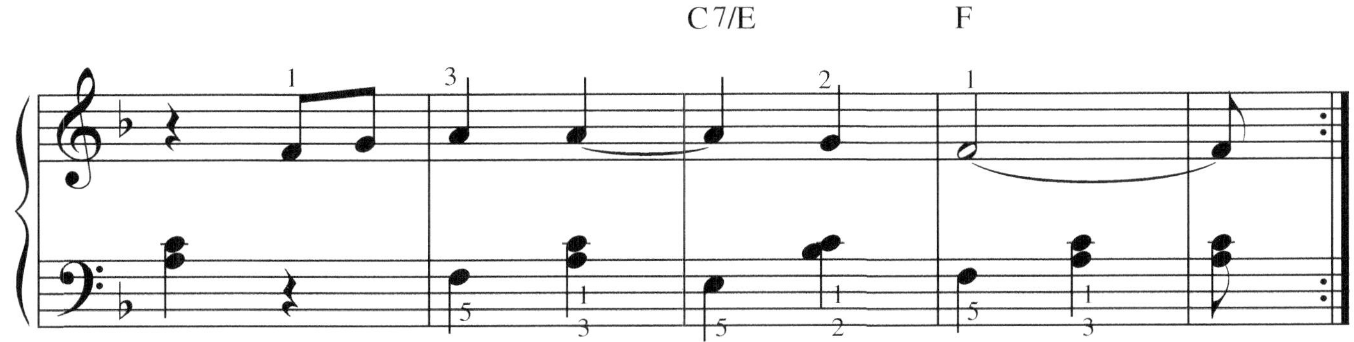

Kumbaya

United States (1926)

Unknown composer
Arr. Bobby Cyr

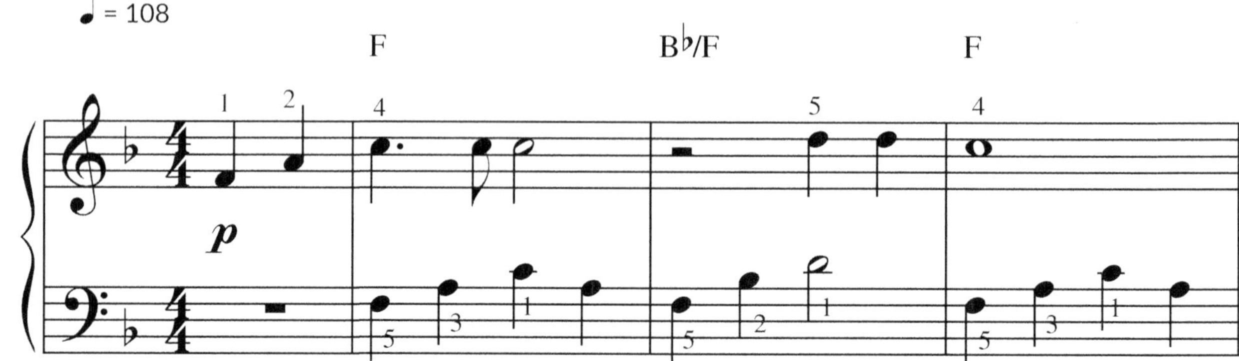

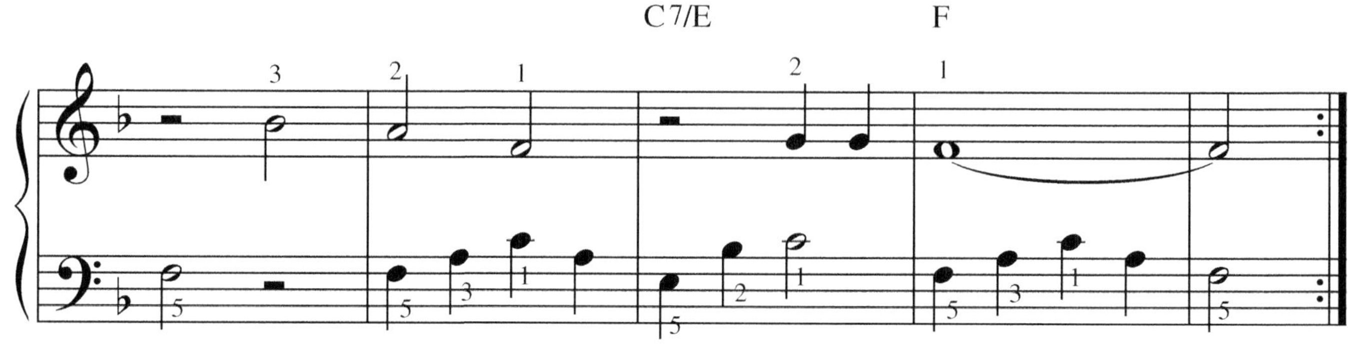

Jimmy Crack Corn

Blue Tail Fly
United States (1846)

Unknown composer
Roud 1274
Arr. Bobby Cyr

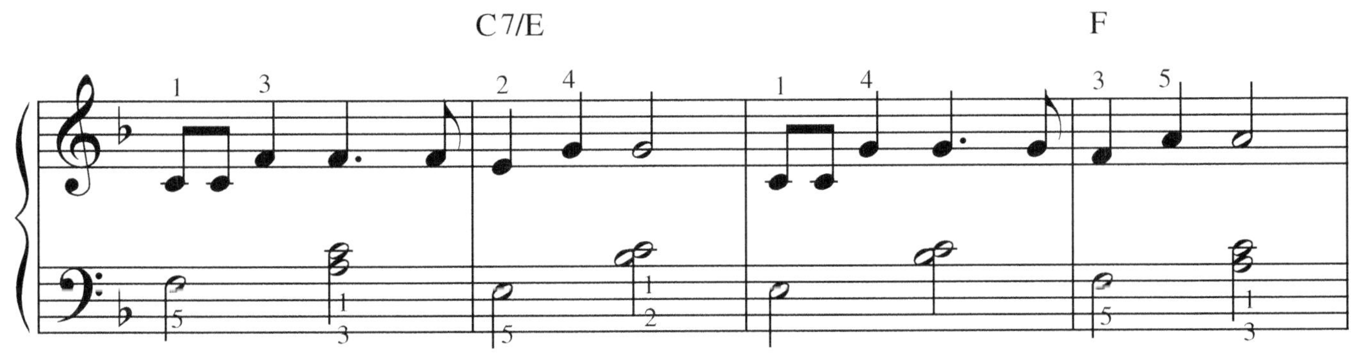

For He's a Jolly Good Fellow

Marlbrough s'en va-t'en guerre
France (1709)

Unknown composer
Arr. Bobby Cyr

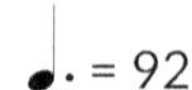

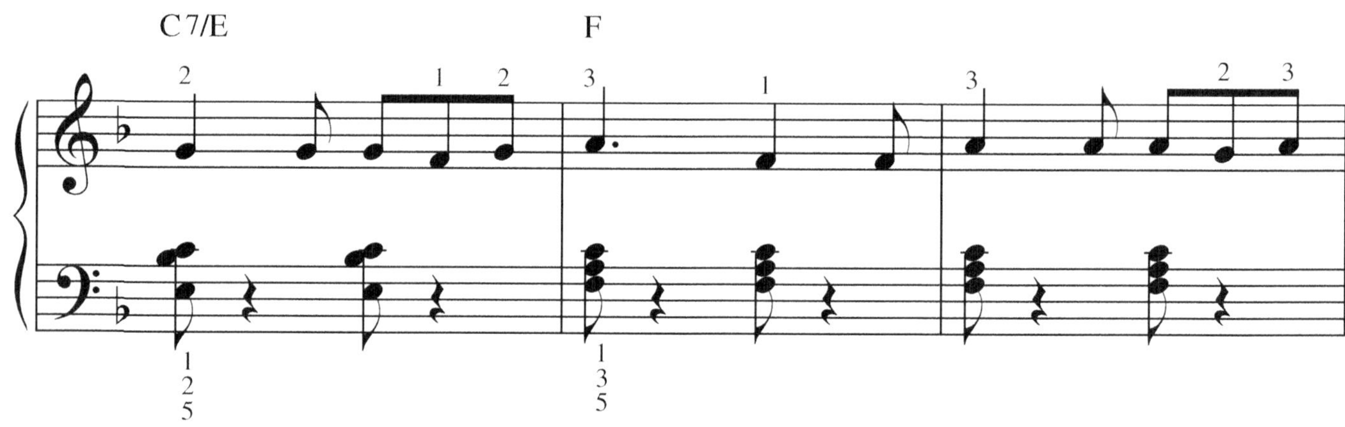

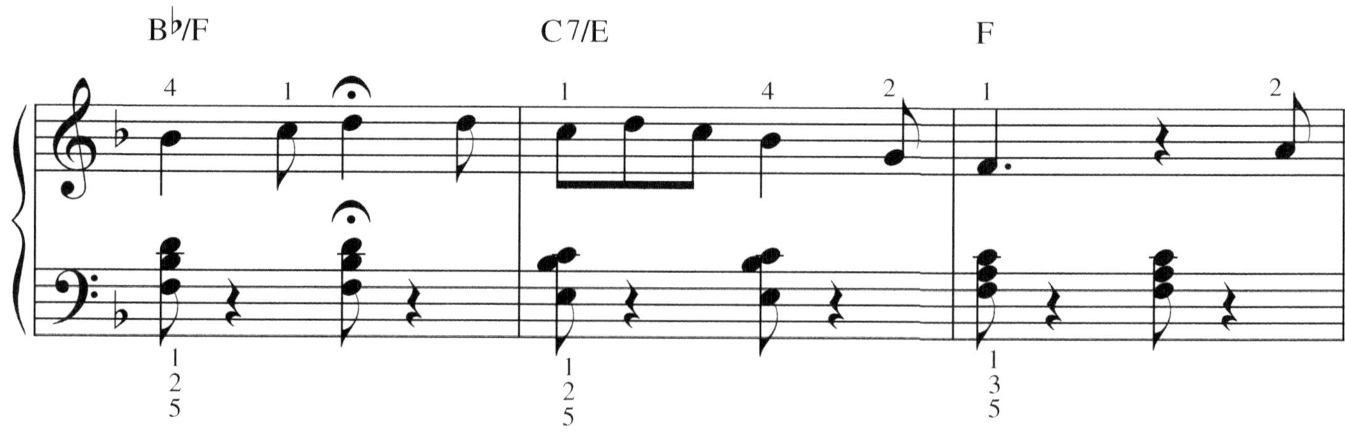

For He's a Jolly Good Fellow

G major

A key signature with one sharp (F sharp) indicates that the piece is in G major.
To fully understand the key of G major, play the G scale and take note of the F sharp.

For more key signatures see: Appendix 3 (page84)

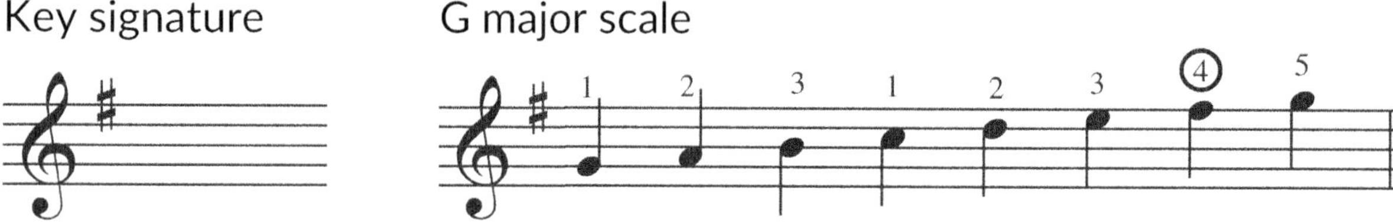

G major chord (G)

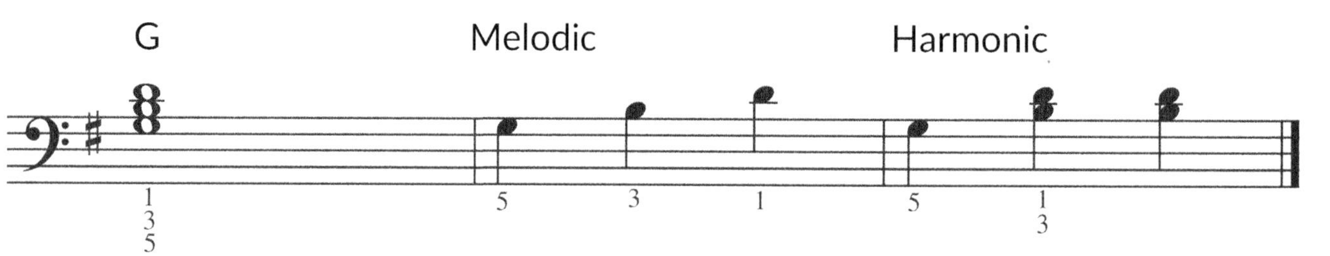

D7 chord with F# as the bass (D7/F#)

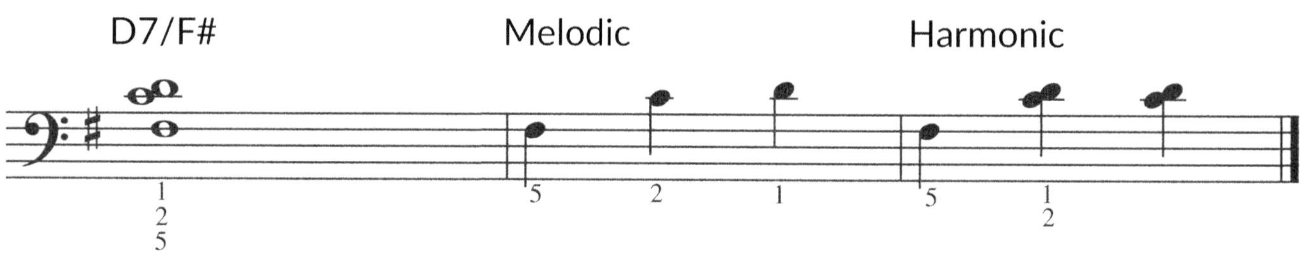

C major chord with G as the bass (C/G)

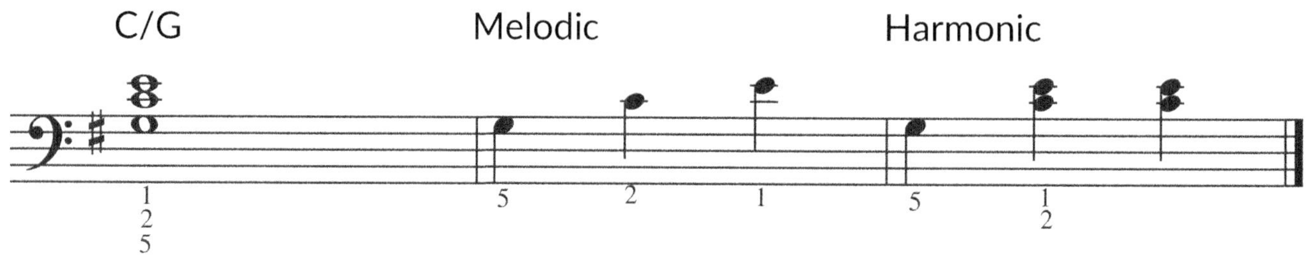

Buffalo Gals

Lubly Fan
United States (1844)

John Hodges
(1821-1891)
Arr. Bobby Cyr

French Can Can

Orphée aux Enfers
France (1858)

Jacques Offenbach
(1819-1880)
Arr. Bobby Cyr

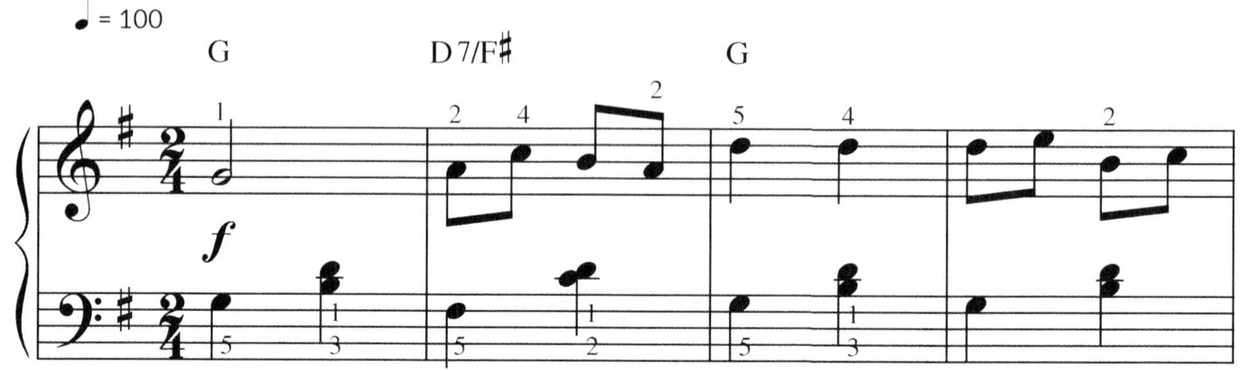

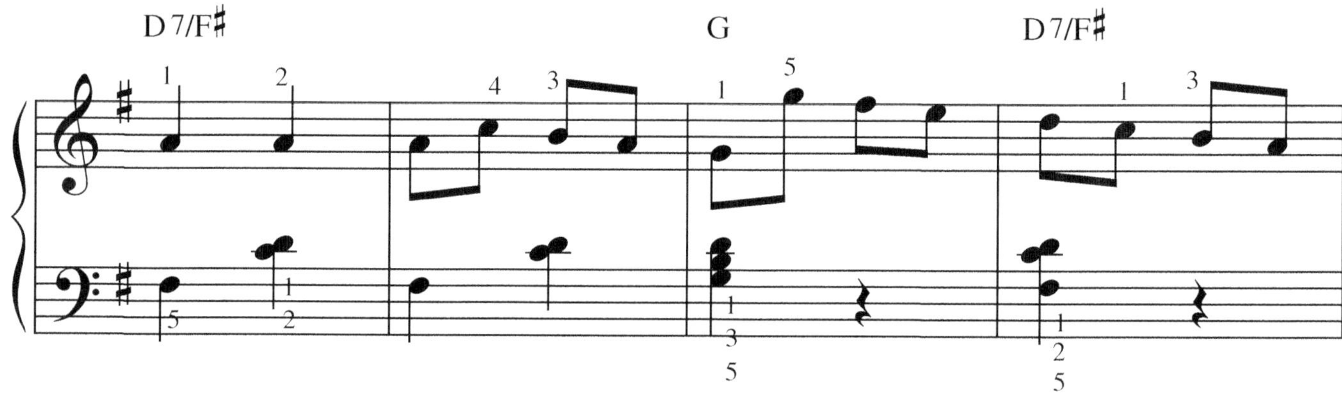

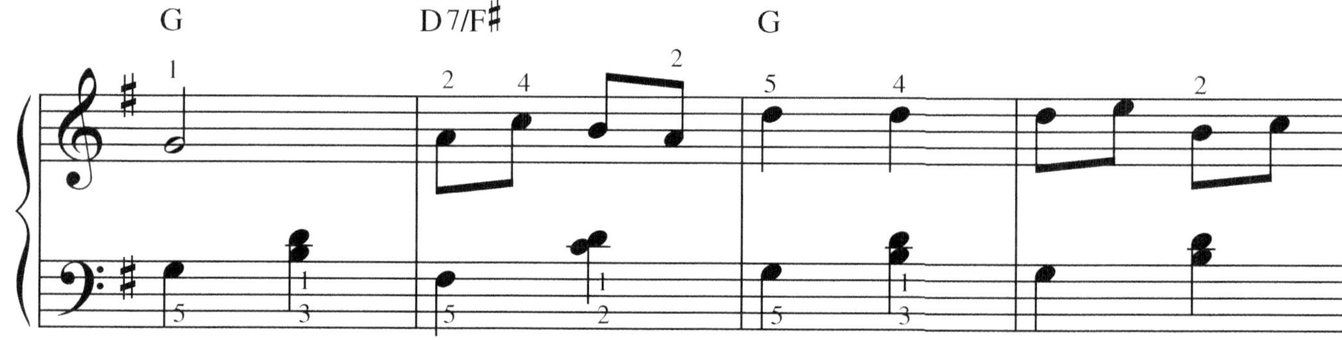

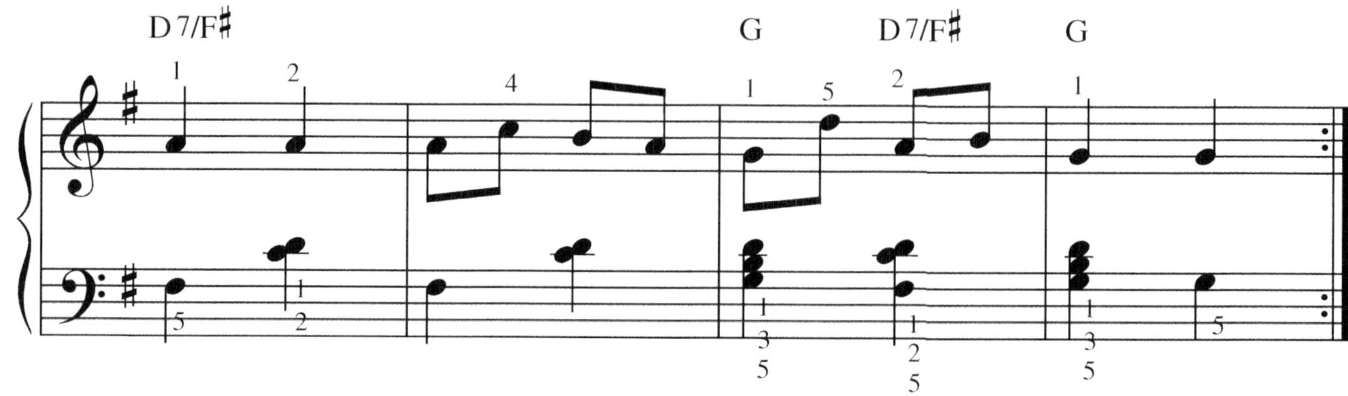

Red River Valley

United States (1896)

Unknown composer
Roud 756
Arr. Bobby Cyr

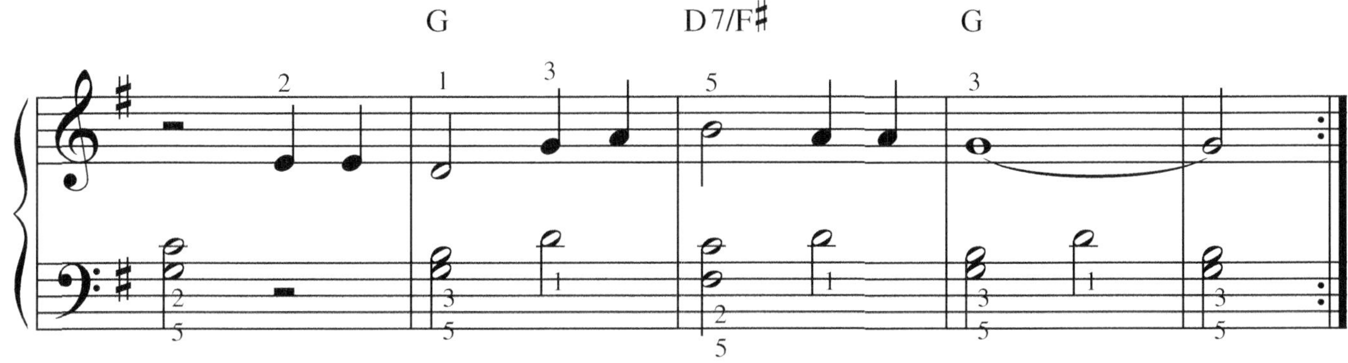

I' ll Tell Me Ma

England (1890)

Unknown composer
Roud 2649
Arr. Bobby Cyr

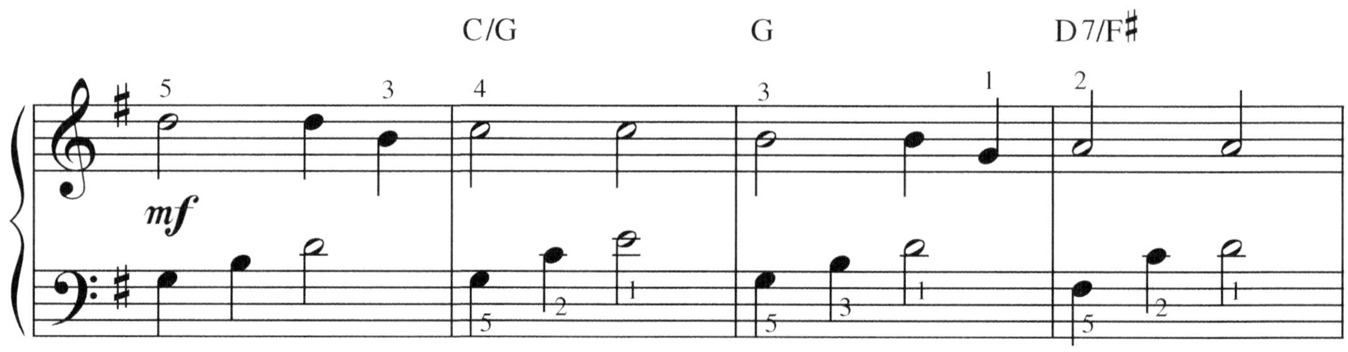

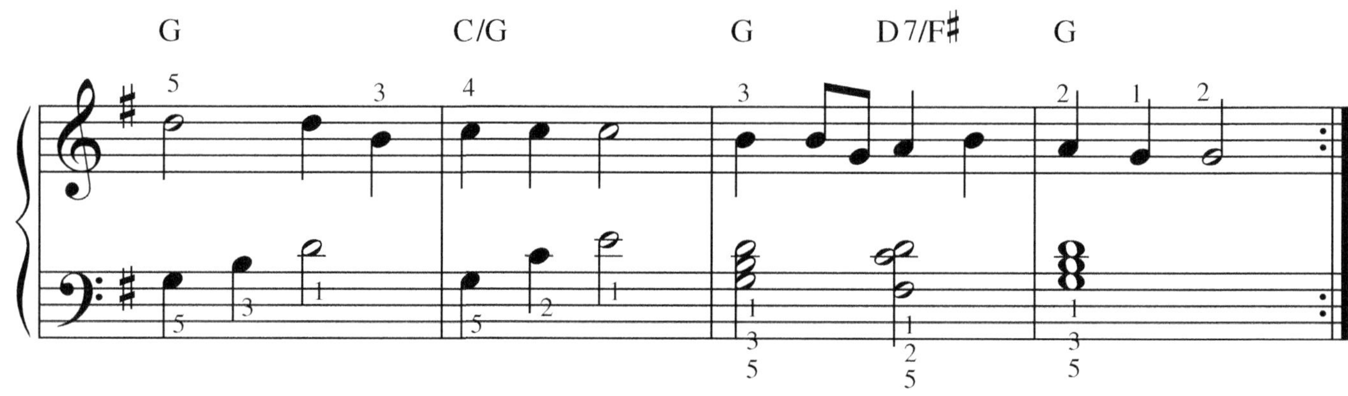

Bonnie Blue Eyes

United States (1914)

Unknown composer
Roud 762
Arr. Bobby Cyr

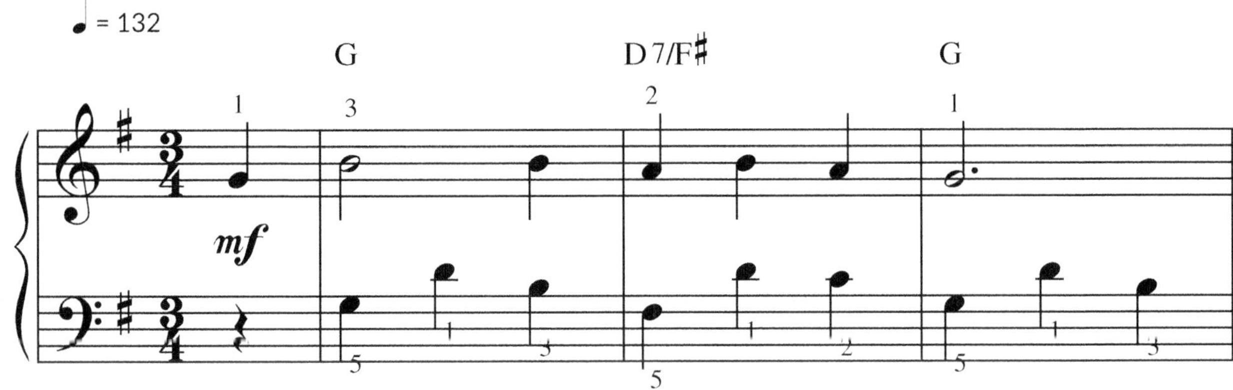

D major chord (D)

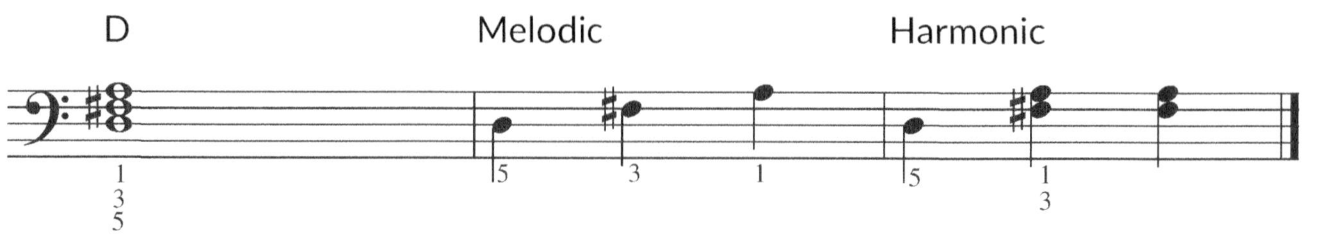

G major chord with D as the bass (G/D)

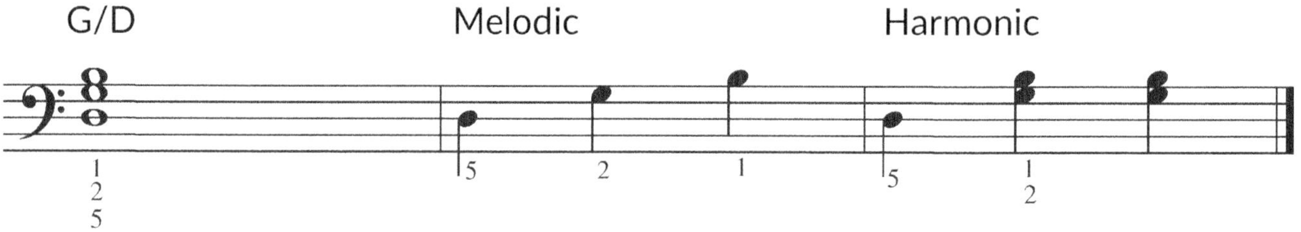

G/D

Melodic

Harmonic

Galway Bay

Ireland (1844)

Frank A. Fahy
(1854–1935)
Arr. Bobby Cyr

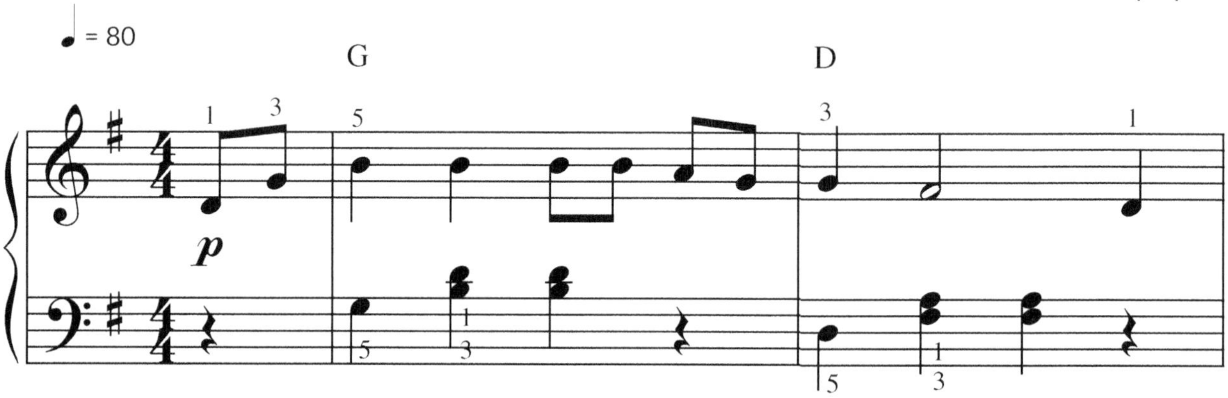

♩ = 80

G

D

p

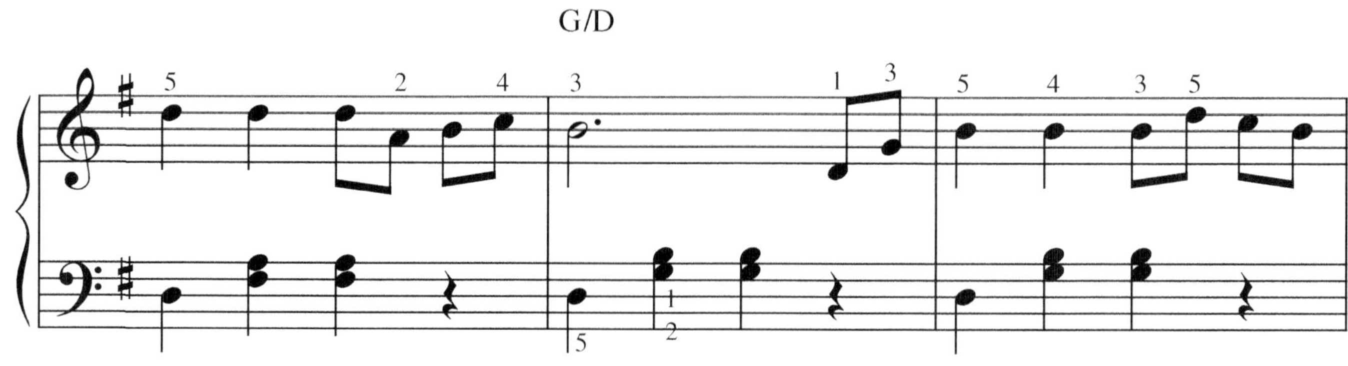

Galway Bay

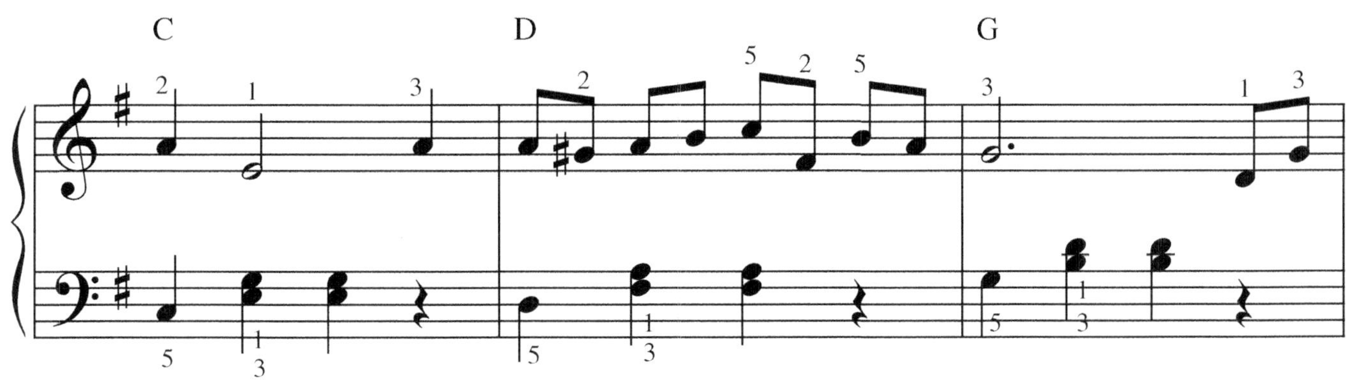

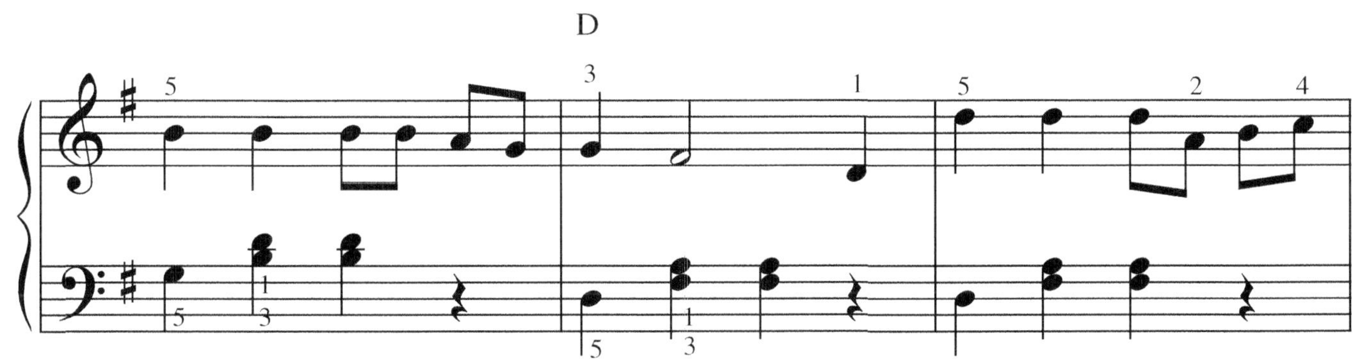

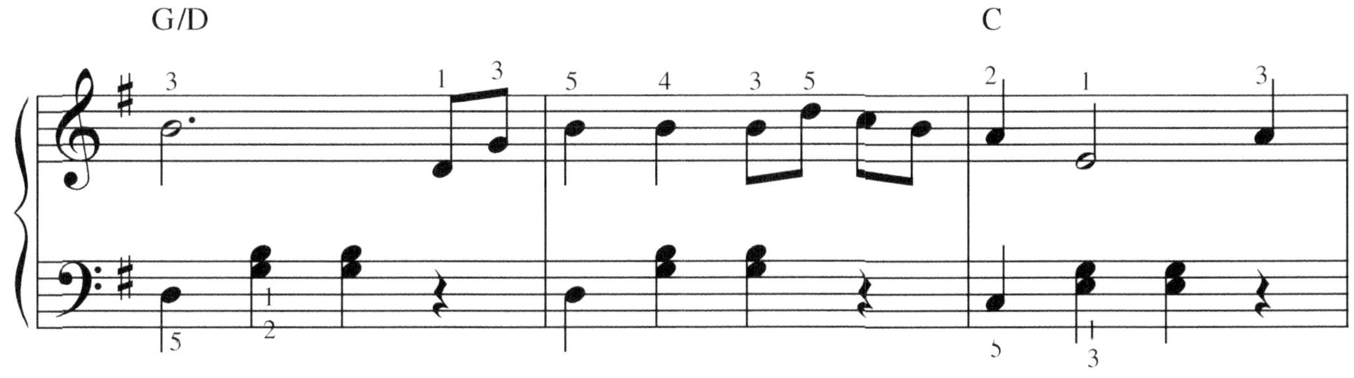

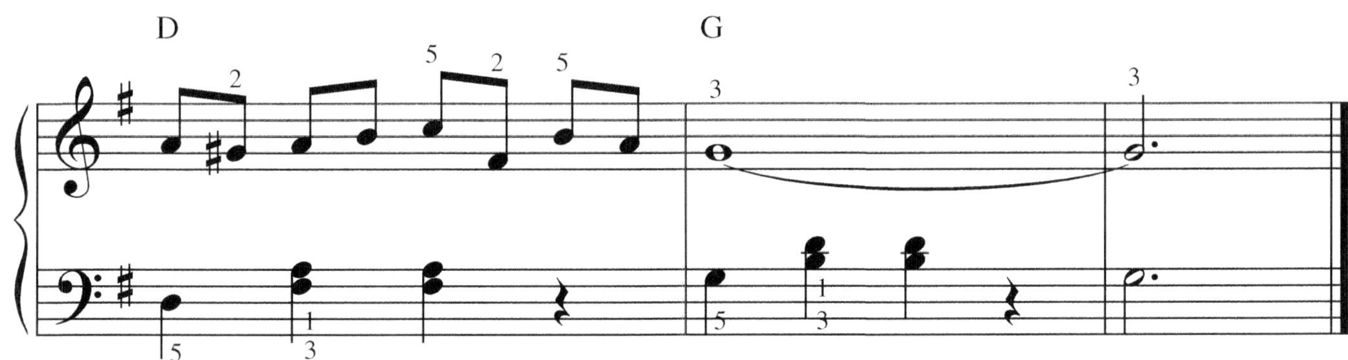

Wabash Cannonball

United States (1882)

J. A. Roff
Arr. Bobby Cyr

Wabash Cannonball

Alberti bass

The Alberti bass pattern is an accompaniment that was used mainly during the Classical period.

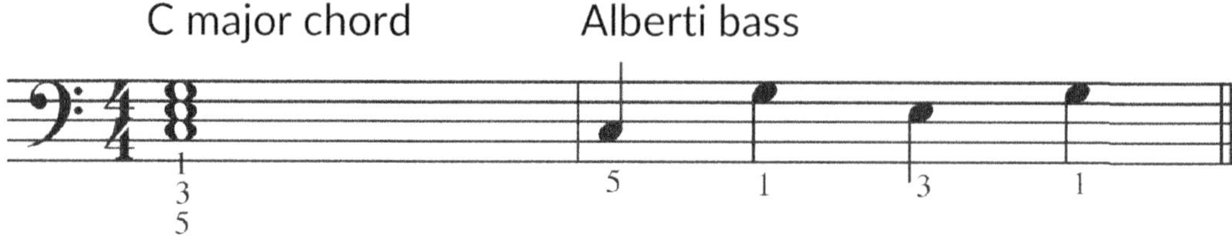

Little Brown Jug

United States (1869)

Joseph Eastburn Winner
(1837-1918)
Arr. Bobby Cyr

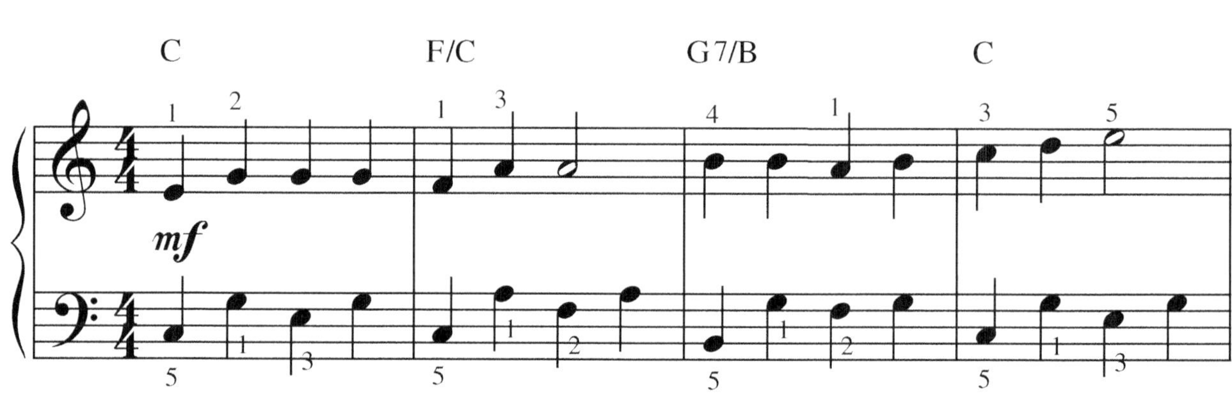

Yalo Yalo

Greece

Unknown composer
Arr. Bobby Cyr

On The Road to Louviers

Sur la route de Louviers
France (1820)

Unknown composer
Arr. Bobby Cyr

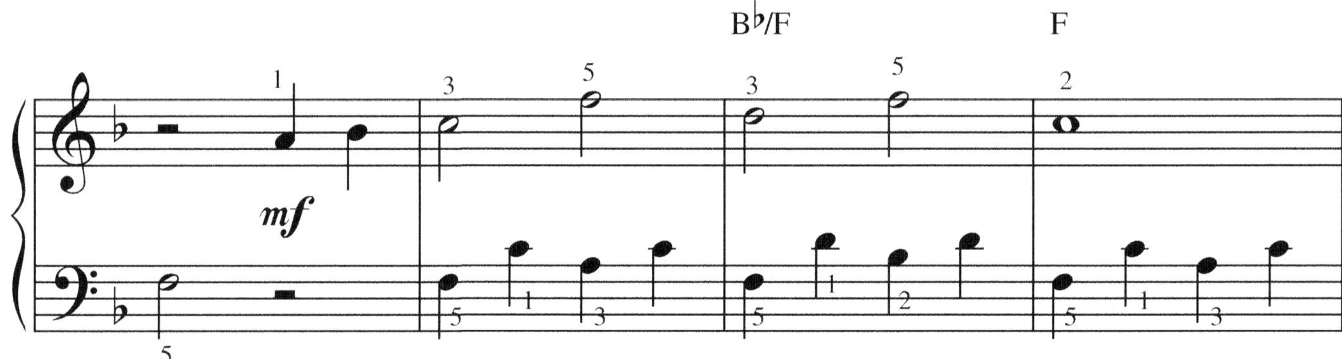

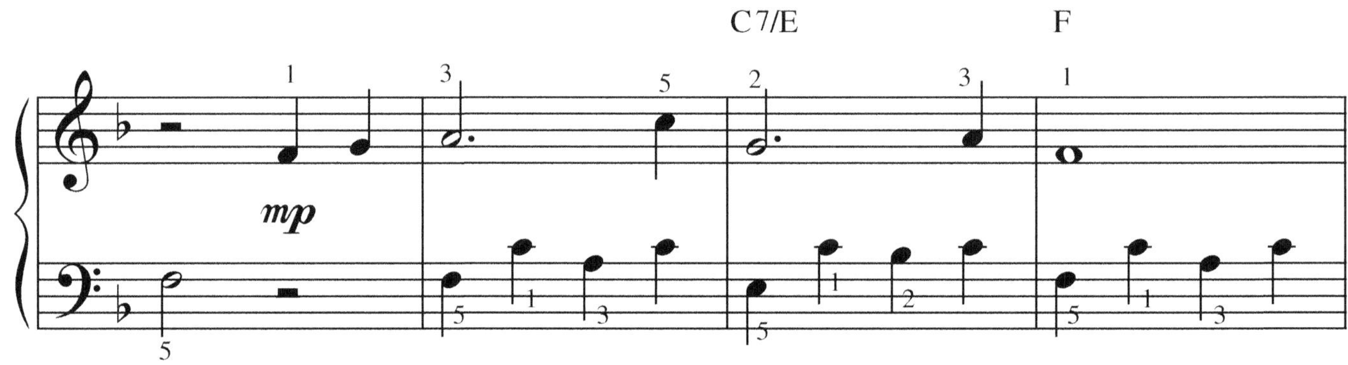

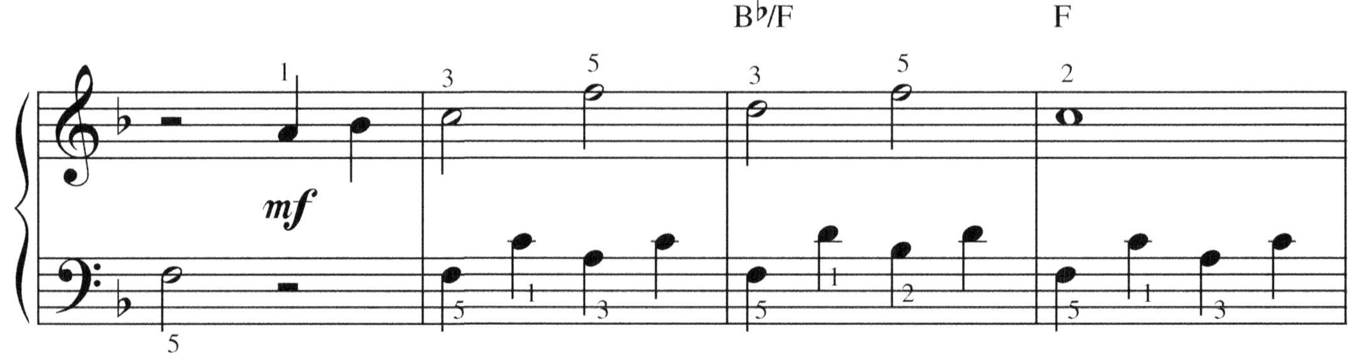

On The Road to Louviers

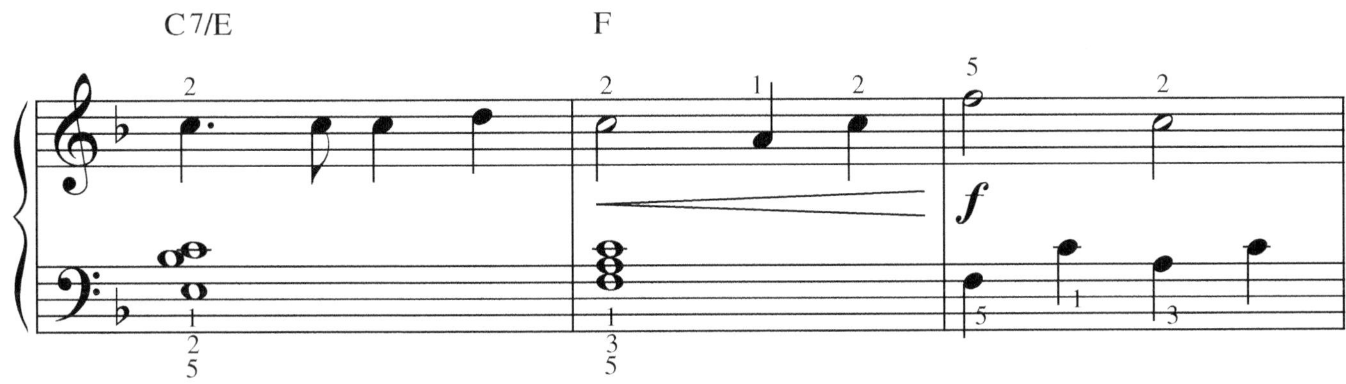

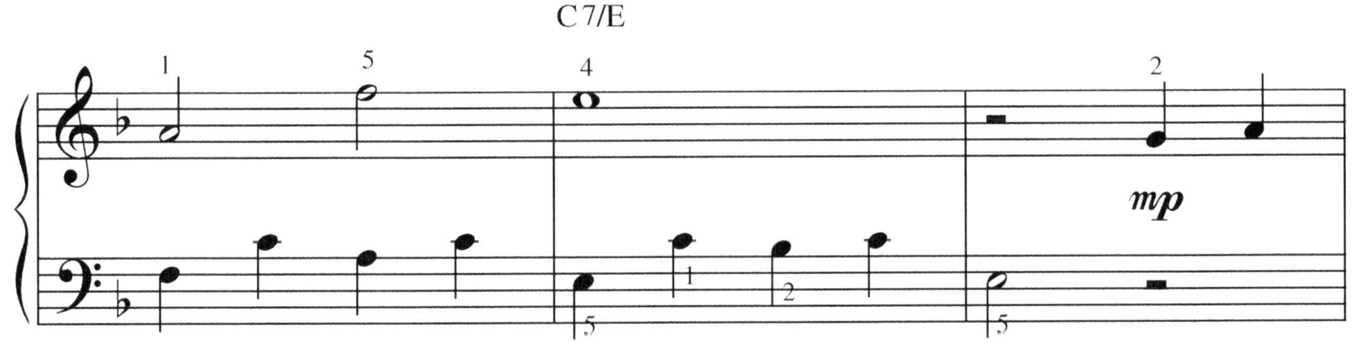

Country Gardens

England (1895)

Unknown composer
Roud 13230
Arr. Bobby Cyr

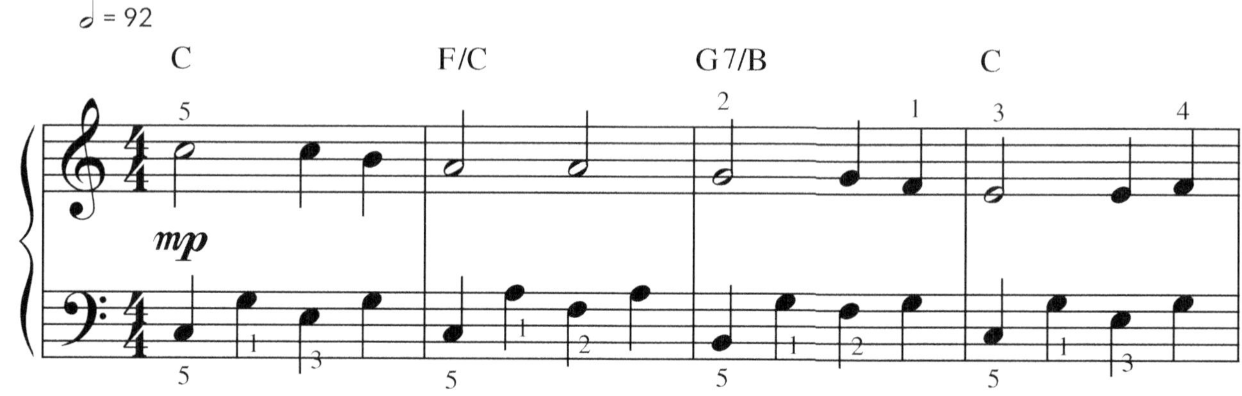

Country Gardens

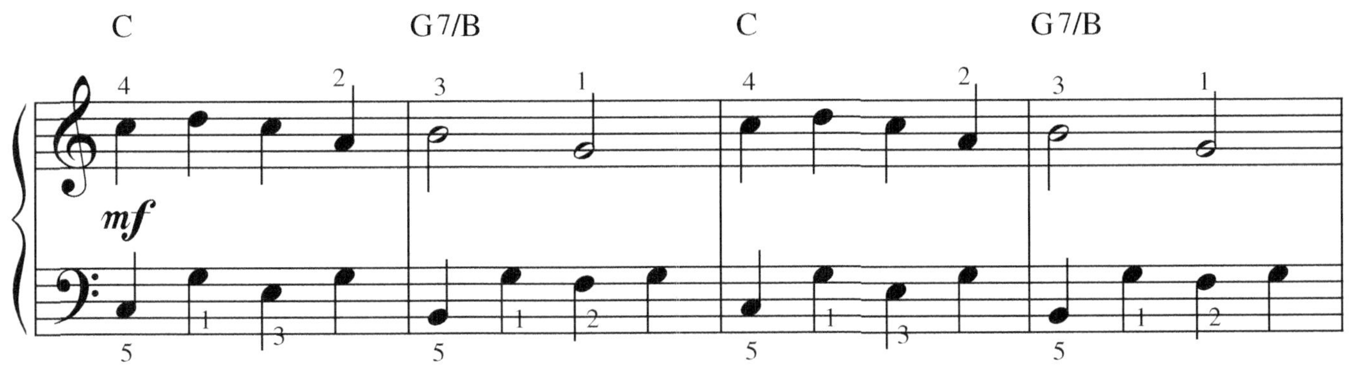

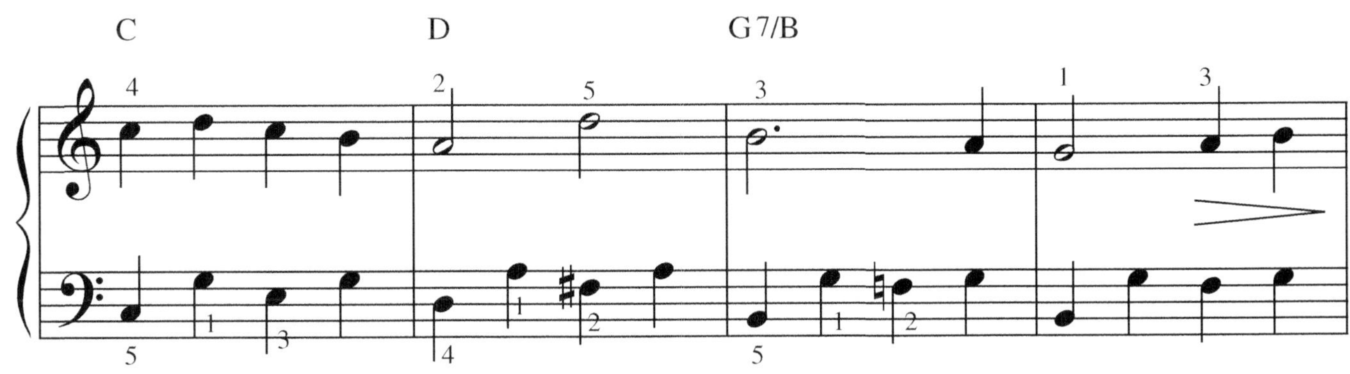

Appendix 1: Reading rhythms

Concepts for rhythm exercise no. 8

Dotted quarter notes | Dotted crotchets

A dotted quarter note has a value equal to a quarter note tied to an eighth note.
The dot adds half of the value of the note to itself.

= Or =

Clap the rhythm and count the beats out loud.

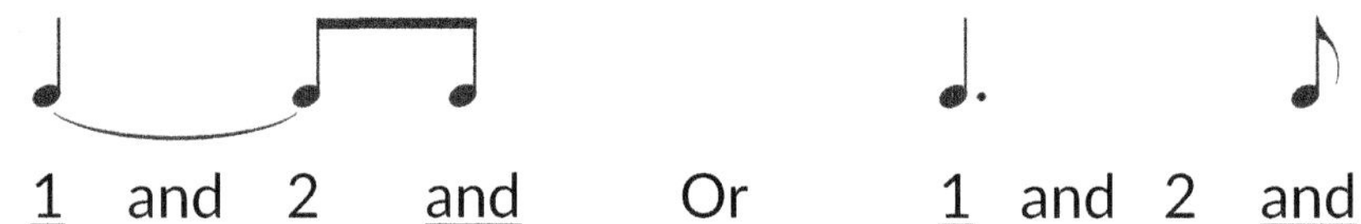

Clap the rhythm and count the beats out loud.
Say (and) between each beat.
Then say (and) silently in your head to master dotted quarter notes.

Rhythm exercise no. 8 (dotted quarter notes | dotted crotchets)

Appendix 1.1

Concepts for rhythm exercise no. 9

Eighth note rests | Quaver rests

An eighth note rest is equal to the value of an eighth note.

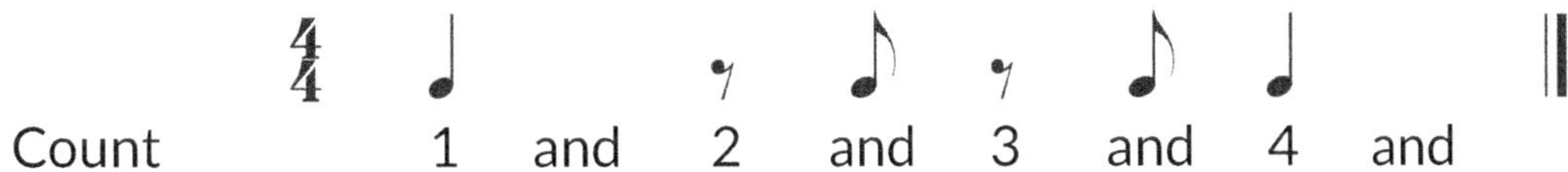

Clap the rhythm and count the beats out loud.
Say (and) between each beat.
Then say (and) silently in your head to master eighth note rests.

Rhythm exercise no. 9 (eighth note rests | Quaver rests)

Appendix 1.2

Concepts for rhythm exercise no. 10

Ternary rhythm | Compound Time

In the 6/8 time signature, the value of each note is doubled.

♪ = 1 beat ♩ = 2 beats ♩. = 3 beats 𝅗𝅥. = 6 beats

There are 6 beats per measure, grouped into 2 groups of 3 eighth notes.
The metronome marking refers to a dotted quarter note.

A tempo marking of 100 for each dotted quarter note is equal to 300 per eighth note.

♩. = 100 equals ♪ = 300

Clap the rhythm and count the beats out loud.

Rhythm exercise no. 10 (6/8 time signature)

Appendix 2: Whole steps and half steps

Whole steps and half steps | Tones and semitones

Whole steps and half steps (tones and semitones) are the smallest musical intervals.

Half steps | Semitones

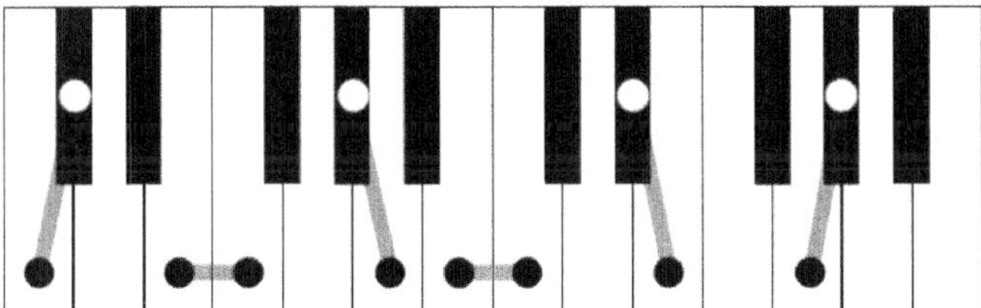

Whole steps | Tones

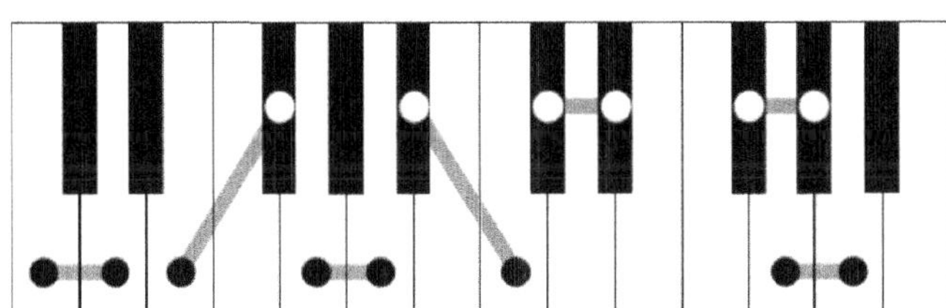

Major scales

A major scale consists of a series of consecutive notes that has a specific interval pattern.
Major scale interval pattern: **tone, tone, semitone, tone, tone, tone, semitone.**

C major scale on the piano.

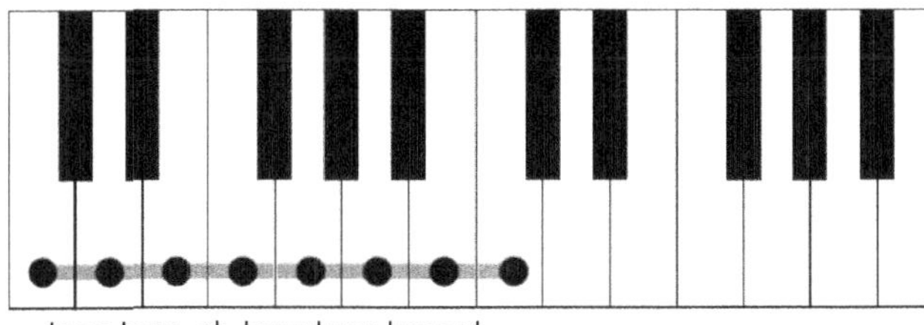

D major scale on the piano.

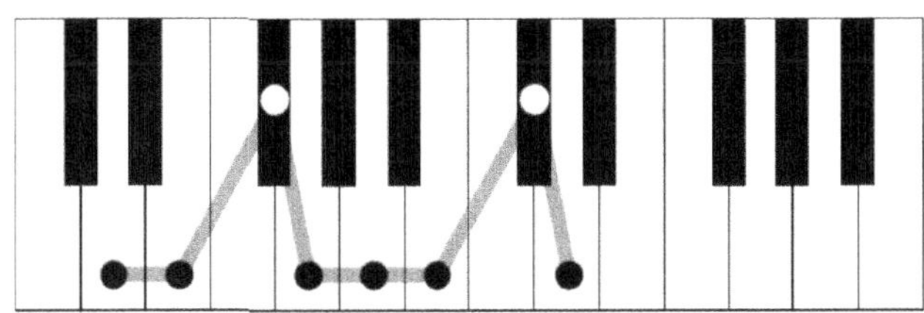

F major scale on the piano.

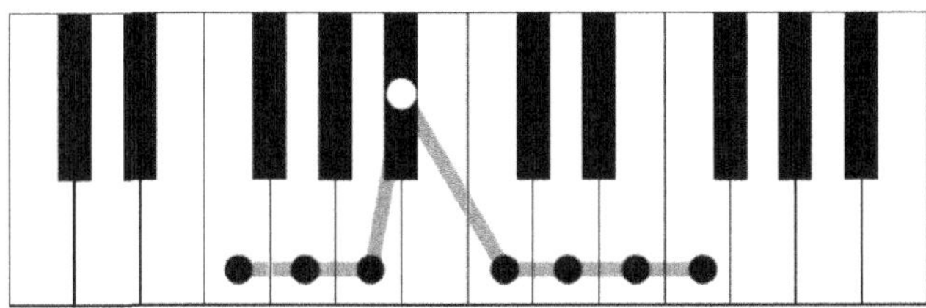

G major scale on the piano.

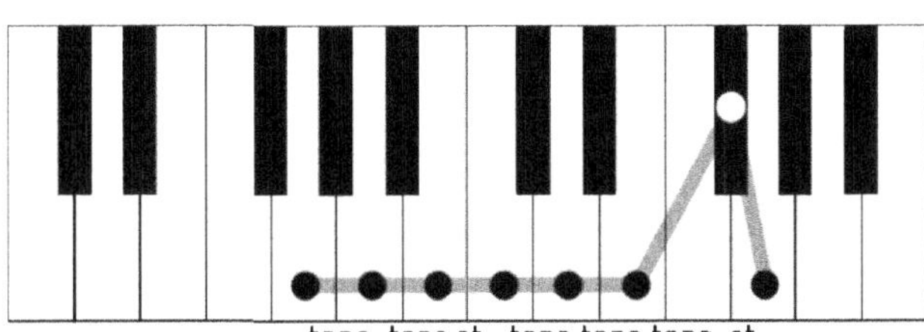

Appendix 2.1: Chord structure

Major chords

A major chord is composed of three notes (a triad): the root, a major third (4 semitones) and a perfect fifth (7 semitones above the root of the chord).
Example of the C major chord: C, E, G

Minor chords

A minor chord contains the root, a minor third (3 semi tones) and a perfect fifth (7 semitones above the root of the chord).
Example of the C minor (Cm) chord: C, E♭, G

Dominant seventh chords

A dominant seventh chord is composed of a major triad with an additional minor seventh (10 semitones above the root of the chord).
Example of the C7 chord: C, E, G, B♭

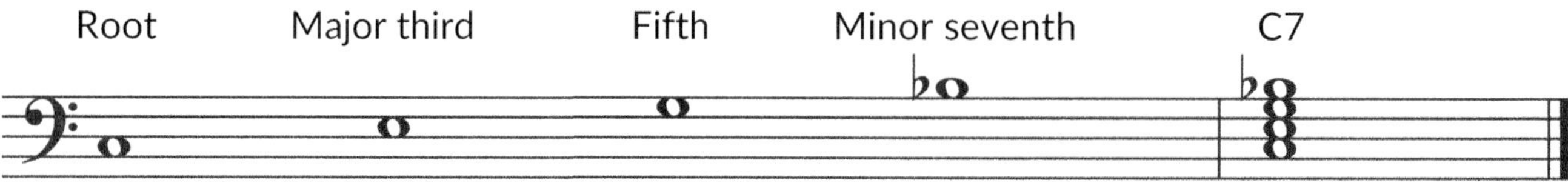

Appendix 2.2: Chord inversions

Three-note chord inversions (triads)

A chord is in root position when the root (or tonic) is the lowest note (or bass note) in the chord. Example of the G chord: G, B, D

When a chord is not in root position, (the root is not the lowest note), it is an inverted chord.

In the first inversion, the third of the triad is the lowest note: B, D, G
In the second inversion, the fifth of the triad is the lowest note: D, G, B

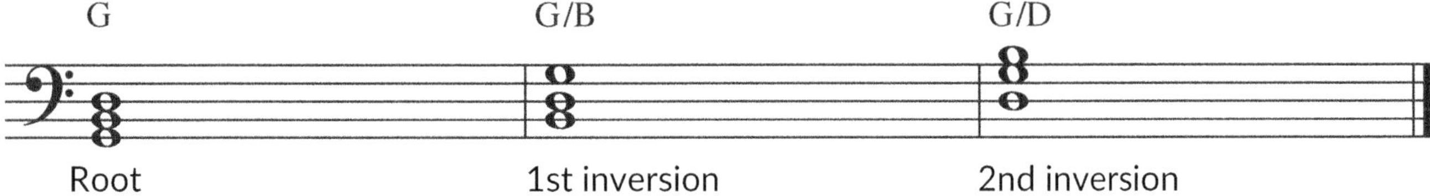

Four-note chord inversions

Four-note chords have an additional third inversion, which happens when the seventh of the chord is the lowest note.

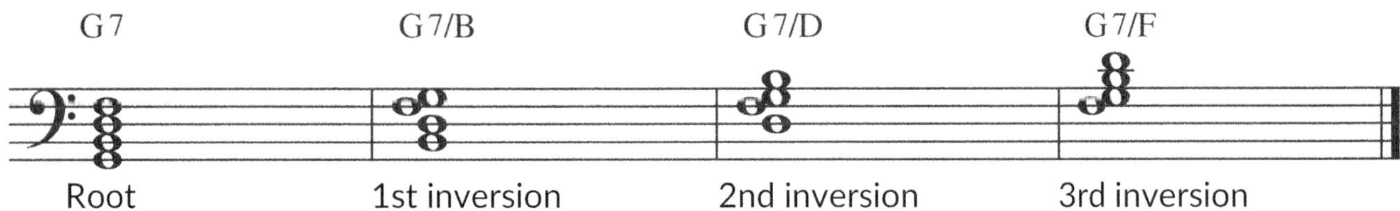

How the G7/B chord is used in this book:

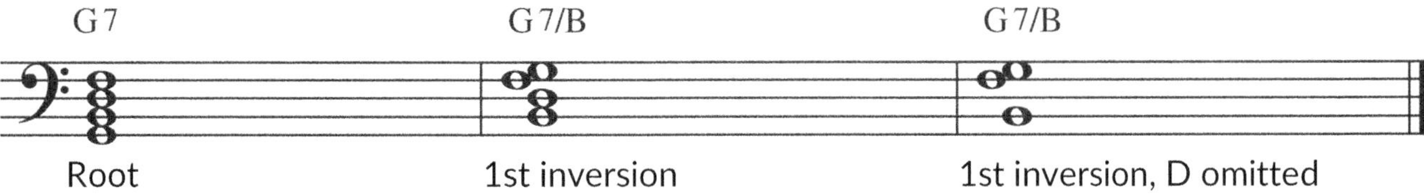

Appendix 3 : Key signatures and scales

Key signatures	Scales	Number of ♯	Order of ♯
	C	-	-
	G	1	F
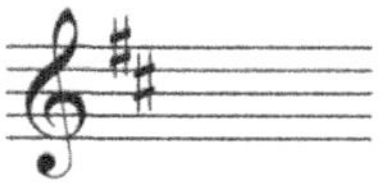	D	2	F, C
	A	3	F, C, G
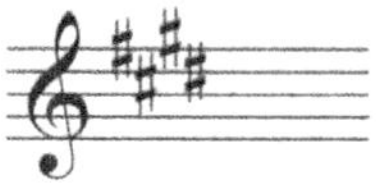	E	4	F, C, G, D
	B	5	F, C, G, D, A
	F♯	6	F, C, G, D, A, E
	C♯	7	F, C, G, D, A, E, B

Key signatures	Scales	Number of ♭	Order of ♭
	F	1	B
	B♭	2	B, E
	E♭	3	B, E, A
	A♭	4	B, E, A, D
	D♭	5	B, E, A, D, G
	G♭	6	B, E, A, D, G, C
	C♭	7	B, E, A D, G, C, F

Concepts learned in Piano Notion Book Two

Flats (♭) sharps (♯) naturals (♮)

Rhythm: dotted quarter note followed by an eighth note  

Intervals and harmony

Major and minor chords

C major arpeggio played with the right hand

Eighth note rests 𝄾

Time signature $\frac{6}{8}$

F major key signature and G major key signature

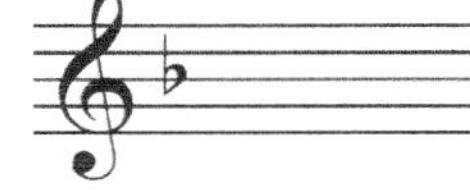 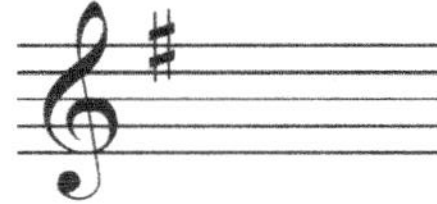

Alberti bass

Certificate of Achievement

This document certifies that

____

Student's name

completed Book Two of the Piano Notion method

On ______________________ ______________________

Date Teacher's name

Congratulations !

Printed in Great Britain
by Amazon

18447528R00052